PARIS
Like a Local

BY THE PEOPLE WHO CALL IT HOME

Contents

6   Welcome to the City
8   Through the Year
10 Know-How
14 Neighbourhoods
16 On the Map

EAT

32 Perfect Patisseries
36 Lunch on the Go
40 Cosy Dinners
44 Top Formules
48 Veggie and Vegan
52 Take a Tour: A morning
    of food in the 12th

DRINK

56 Coffee Shops
60 Wine Bars
64 Cocktail Joints
68 Breweries and Wineries
72 Unmissable Terraces
76 Take a Tour: An evening
    of cocktail culture

SHOP

80 Gourmet Treats
84 Beloved Markets
88 Home Touches
92 Books and Stationery
96 Street Style
100 Beauty Buys
104 Take a Tour: An afternoon
    of haute couture

ARTS & CULTURE

108 Museum Lates
112 Modern Art
116 Esoteric Collections
120 On Stage and Screen
124 City History
128 Community Projects
132 Take a Tour: An afternoon
    exploring Paris's art scene

NIGHTLIFE

136 Guinguettes and Rooftops

140 Music Nights

144 Game Night

148 Open-air Living Rooms

152 Apéritif Spots

156 Take a Tour: An evening following the Seine path

OUTDOORS

160 Picnic Spots

164 Urban Adventures

168 By the Water

172 Dreamy Viewpoints

176 Streets and Squares

180 Nearby Getaways

184 Take a Tour: A morning flânerie through edgy Belleville

186 Directory

188 Index

192 Acknowledgments

meet the locals

YUKI HIGASHINAKANO

Born in Tokyo and raised in Paris's suburbs, Yuki is always finding new pockets of the city to fall in love with. A cultural coordinator by day, Yuki spends time browsing cosy bookshops, searching for the next community kitchen to volunteer at and living to eat (well, it's easy to in Paris).

BRYAN PIROLLI

Now Brooklyn-based, Bryan spent over a decade living in Paris, earning his PhD at the Sorbonne and French citizenship all in the same year. When he's back in Paris and not writing, teaching university students or running his LGBTQ+ tour company, he finds time to picnic along the canal and cruise the Haussmannian avenues atop his trusty cycle, Pierre-Auguste.

Paris

WELCOME TO THE CITY

Few people are prouder of their city than Parisians – or quicker to defend its quirks. Life here is lived intensely and fiercely, with a real sense of community in each *quartier*: long-time street sellers ply their trade rain or shine, and few days pass without the simple pleasures of a lazy coffee, or a debate with friends over good food. Calling the city home means making sacrifices – not least when it comes to apartment space – but locals are repaid tenfold in having Europe's best restaurants on their doorstep. Parisians might be famously haughty and aloof, but they've got reason to believe their *mode de vie* is the best in the world.

It's easy to see why Paris inspires so many: the city is inarguably beautiful. Yet while defined by Haussmannian façades and romantic vistas, it's not homogenous. You might fall in love with the multicultural areas in the outer arrondissements where run-down bars still serve tiny espressos or with an up-and-coming suburb like Pantin. But no matter where you are, tradition holds strong. Picking up a still-warm baguette before dinner or ending the work day with a pavement-table *apéro* are necessities, not clichés.

There are, however, some clichés that locals roll their eyes at, and that's where this book comes in. We know what Parisians cherish the most, and we've brought together the people and places shaping the city's future. While it's impossible to wholly encapsulate Paris in these pages, you'll find a snapshot of its diversity. That means counter-cultural community projects, esoteric art collections, and where to find the best street markets and street style.

Whether you consider yourself a Parisian and want to unearth your city's secrets or you're looking for inspiration for your first trip, this book will help you to delve deeper. Don't settle for the best-known boulevards and brasseries. See Paris, but do it the local way.

Liked by the locals

"Sure, you'll get the Paris that you see in the movies. But the true magic of this city is in finding your own corner, an enchanting place that you feel is made just for you."

YUKI HIGASHINAKANO,
CULTURAL COORDINATOR

From sultry summer parties to wintry wanders through festive markets, each season brings with it a new lease of cultural life in Paris.

Paris
THROUGH THE YEAR

SPRING

THE GREAT OUTDOORS

As life unfurls after winter, pavement terraces spring back and days are spent watching the world go by with a coffee.

TRADITIONAL FESTIVALS

Marking the transition from winter to spring are city-wide celebrations. Riotous dragon parades kick off Chinese New Year while chapel concerts and long dinners define family time around Easter.

GAME, SET, MATCH

Parisians can't wait for the French Tennis Open in May. Avid fans book tickets to catch a game at the stadium, but most locals gather with pals at a sports bar to watch it live on screen.

PARIS IN BLOOM

Fresh flowers and cherry blossom start to line the banks of the Seine and the big parks in April, resulting in the first picnics of the year: a Parisian pastime.

SUMMER

FESTIVAL FUN

Parisians never need an excuse to party, and June is prime time for it. The Fête de la Musique sees musicians take to the streets, Pride offers up a carnival-like parade and a jazz festival gets everyone swaying. After-parties are custom, too.

ALFRESCO LIVING

Warmer weather sees life move outdoors. On sunny days, Parisians cool off along the banks of the Seine and the Bassin de la Villette, which are transformed into "beaches" for Paris-Plages. Balmy nights are spent hanging out along the canal and dancing at rooftop bars.

BASTILLE DAY
The city's fire stations throw infamous champagne-fuelled parties (aka the *bal des pompiers*) the night before Bastille Day. Those not too hungover line the Seine the next day to watch the 14 juillet fireworks or catch the Military Parade.

AUTUMN
CULTURAL TOURS
Parisians dread *la rentrée* (the return), when vacations end and schools go back in September. Keeping spirits high is the start of a new cultural season. Exhibitions and plays launch, and the Nuit Blanche in October offers up an all-night party of gallery events.

HARVEST TIME
Autumn brings with it the start of the wine harvest season, and wine-loving locals flock to dedicated events. Restaurants and bars also celebrate with tastings, special menus and the odd accordion player to entertain.

COSY DINNERS
When the first cold breeze arrives, comfort food is the perfect antidote. Dinner parties are hosted and friends gather in restaurants for raclette.

CHILLY NIGHTS
Parisians resist retreating inside until the end of autumn, drawing terrace season out into November, with restaurants and bars offering cozy blankets.

WINTER
SPARKLY WONDERLAND
The City of Lights literally lights up to mark the start of the Christmas period, with extravagant shop displays and illuminated trees in pretty gardens.

MARKETS GALORE
Every Parisian has either gifted, or been gifted, a trinket from one of the city's Christmas markets. But it's about more than shopping, with funfair rides, traditional stalls and gourmet treats.

WINTER SALES
Fashionistas wait all year for January, when *Les Soldes* are in full swing and sales tempt the renewal of wardrobes.

There's an art to being a Parisian, from the dos and don'ts of café culture to negotiating the city's busiest streets. Here's a breakdown of all you need to know.

Paris

KNOW-HOW

For a directory of health and safety resources, safe spaces, and accessibility information, turn to page 186. For everything else, read on.

EAT

Sitting down for a meal is sacred in Paris. Most Parisians take a full hour for lunch, served from 12pm to 2pm, and tend to order a *formule* (set menu). If you need a quick bite, find a place to perch: locals don't eat as they walk. Dinners are also relaxed and start with an apéritif (pre-dinner drink), with food ready no earlier than 8pm. As mealtimes are cherished, it's key to book ahead; note that many places close on Sundays and Mondays.

DRINK

Drinking on an outdoor *terrasse* is a ritual in Paris, where café-bars are packed from the first espresso through to the last beers around 2am. As such, coffee to go isn't the norm; if you need a quick flat white, go to a speciality coffee shop.

Don't wait to be seated: draw up a chair at a table without cutlery and staff will come to take your order. Wine and beer are acceptable from noon, but you'll raise eyebrows if you order an apéritif such as a spritz after dinner. Often there's no menu: just ask for what you want.

SHOP

There's one rule to follow wherever you're shopping: say *bonjour* (hello) when you arrive and *bonne journée* (have a good day) when you leave. Many Parisians find the failure to follow these niceties very rude and offer haughty service in return. At flea markets, haggling is accepted (for the expensive items, that is – don't bother on a €5 trinket box). As you now know, lunch is a sacred time, and smaller businesses may close from around 1 to 3pm. Oh, and carry a tote bag to avoid a plastic bag charge.

ARTS & CULTURE

Most museums and galleries are, wonderfully, free to EU citizens under 26; otherwise, tickets cost around €10–15. There's usually an extra charge for the latest temporary exhibitions – a staple in many calendars. If you go to the theatre, dress smartly and carry at least €2 to tip the usher who shows you to your seat.

NIGHTLIFE

As dinners tend to end around 10–11pm (and later on the weekend), Parisians don't get serious about entertainment until late. Clubs and music venues get going around midnight, and many bars stay open until 2am. Nights are spent leisurely, whether socializing around a table or outdoors in summer. Despite the number of drinks you consume, it's not seen as acceptable to get inebriated. After-dark Parisian style is pretty casual, too, so there's little need to dress up.

OUTDOORS

Parisians live outside when they can. Picnicking is a much-loved pastime, but permission to sit on the grass isn't a given, so look out for signs before you settle. In summer, the banks of the Seine and the Canal Saint-Martin are packed with locals escaping the heat and relaxing with friends. Wherever you hang out, keep Paris pretty and take rubbish with you.

Keep in mind

Here are some other tips and titbits that will help you fit in like a local.

» **Keep cash handy** Contactless payments are making inroads, but some shops, markets and old-school bars are still cash only.

» **Tip, please** Service is technically included for meals, but most people tip waiters up to 10 per cent. Taxi drivers don't expect a tip.

» **Smoke outside** Smoking is allowed on most *terrasses*; just ask for a *cendrier* (ashtray) and don't drop butts on the floor.

» **Stay hydrated** Paris is home to hundreds of free drinking fountains (some even offer sparkling water), so bring a bottle.

GETTING AROUND

Central Paris is relatively small and divided into 20 arrondissements (districts) that radiate out in a clockwise spiral from the Seine. This river runs through the heart of the city: the north side is known as the Rive Droite (Right Bank), and the south as the Rive Gauche (Left Bank). City limits are defined by the ring road known as the Boulevard Périphérique, or Périph. While neighbourhoods outside this and the centre's "75" zip code are no longer considered "Paris" by locals, many are interesting to explore, from semi-suburbs like Saint-Denis to up-and-coming Pantin.

To make your life easier we've provided what3words addresses for each sight in this book, meaning you can quickly pinpoint exactly where you're heading with ease.

On foot

Central Paris is pretty compact, and you can walk from the likes of the Arc de Triomphe to the Bastille in an hour. Arrondissements are marked on every street sign, so it's hard to get too lost. Aside from the practicalities, though, strolling the city is simply a pleasure; the French even have a name for going on a wander – a *flânerie* – so it all figures. However, don't assume that everyone

is out for a casual stroll: Parisians are busy people, so avoid dawdling on the pavements (especially narrow ones). If you do need to check a what3words location, step to the side.

On wheels

With the exception of Montmartre, Paris is reasonably flat. Add to that many traffic-restricted backstreets and a network of bike lanes, and the city is a cyclist's dream. This is the only time we'll advise you not to do as the locals do: never ride on the pavement (yep, you'll see Parisians do it) and wear a helmet.

The 24-hour pioneering Vélib' scheme set the standard for bike-sharing projects around the world. There are myriad docking stations around the city, with one- or seven-day passes available online. The green bikes (normal) are free to ride for the first 30 minutes, increasing by €1 for every additional half-hour up to €4, while the teal versions (electric) start at €1. *www.velib-metropole.fr*

By public transport

When you need to travel from one side of the city to the other, Paris has you covered. The Métro is pretty quick and runs until 2am at the weekend (plus, its Art Nouveau signage and beautifully designed stations are city emblems). Buses are less glamorous but often handy.

The city's old system of paper tickets is being phased out and replaced with Navigo Travel Cards, which you can pick up at any station. With this card, it's possible to buy a daily or weekly travel pass for use on any form of public transport; you can also pay-as-you-go.

For longer trips, you'll take the RER, a web of underground-overground commuter lines. On all routes, watch out for pickpockets: passports and wallets are routinely snatched. If you're riding an escalator, stand only on the right – Parisians use the left for walking.

By car or taxi

Driving in Paris is not for the faint-hearted – think heavy traffic, one-way streets and scarce parking spots. Few Parisians drive unless heading out of the city; rent a car from Europcar to join them.

Official Taxis Parisiens, distinguished by their green lights, are safe and reliable but generally expensive. You can hail them on the street or head to taxi ranks at the major stations. Other taxi apps include the ubiquitous Uber, FreeNow and G7. They're worth considering for journeys late at night.
www.europcar.co.uk

Download these

We recommend you download these apps to help you get about the city.

WHAT3WORDS
Your geocoding friend

A what3words address is a simple way to communicate any precise location on earth, using just three words. ///spent.spacing.storms, for example, is the code for the famous Louvre Pyramid. Simply download the free what3words app, type a what3words address into the search bar, and you'll know exactly where to go.

RATP
Your local transport service

All public transport in Paris and the wider Île-de-France region is run by the RATP. The official app is great for information straight from the source, including first and last departures of the day. You can also create travel itineraries to work out the most efficient way to reach your destination.

Paris is defined by arrondissements, each made up of village-like neighbourhoods with their own character. Here we take a look at some of our favourites.

Paris

NEIGHBOURHOODS

1st

Parisians might not live in this tourist epicentre (it's where you'll find the Louvre), but they do pop by, weaving around the crowds to pick up lunch from boulangeries and run errands. {map 1}

2nd

It's all about food here, which is fitting since the 2nd was once home to Paris's central food market. These days, the smells of spices and matcha tea tempt foodies along Rue Saint-Anne – or Little Tokyo, a street full of fab Japanese-owned restaurants. {map 1}

3rd

The city's aristocracy once lived in the Haut Marais, so it's pretty fancy. Medieval mansions, upscale galleries and cute cafés lie here, attracting chic locals who all drop by to be seen. {map 2}

4th

A Jewish quarter since the 19th century, Le Marais is one of the city's most multicultural areas. (Note: you won't find better falafel than in the 4th.) It's buzzing too, thanks to an influx of LGBTQ+ bars and shops since the 1990s. {map 2}

5th

Bookshops on every block, dive bars and young café crowds – not to mention a quick walk to the Sorbonne University – are enough for students to put down roots in the Latin Quarter. {map 2}

6th

This was the meeting place for writers in the mid-20th century, though it's more of a chichi area today. That said, the historic cafés of Saint Germain remain a heartland for creatives. {map 1}

7th

Forget the 3rd; the 7th is the real exclusive address. Yes, the Eiffel Tower is on the doorstep, but the 7th is also awash with upscale bistros, elegant architecture and a quaint village feel. {map 1}

8th

Famed for its shopping street, the Champs-Élysées, the 8th is where fashionistas scour luxury boutiques and mingle with glam locals. {map 4}

9th

Flagship department stores and top-notch theatres make the 9th a classy area. It's not all elegance, though. Near the Opéra district lies hipster Pigalle, where bars buzz until late. *{map 4}*

10th

Fast gentrifying but still multicultural, with a strong Indian community, the 10th is loved for its local grocery stores, indie coffee shops and the canal, where "bobos" (bohemian-bourgeois Parisians) pass days. *{map 5}*

11th

No other area can match the 11th's foodie scene (sorry, 2nd). Locals journey here to eat at Paris's best restaurants; think hip brunch spots and traditional bistros. *{map 3}*

12th

Ditching its gritty rep, the 12th is on the up – just ask the young families who settle here. Aside from its green spaces, the 12th is famed for the Marché d'Aligre – the perfect place to pick up snacks for picnics. *{map 3}*

13th

Since migrants from Laos, Cambodia, Vietnam and China settled here after the Vietnam War, it's been known as the Asian Quarter. It's still multicultural, home to a fab Chinatown (Europe's largest, but we're not bragging) and, naturally, the best Asian food joints in the city. *{map 6}*

14th

When painters and poets congregated here in the early 20th century, Montparnasse grew into a liberal epicentre. Okay, it's seen modernization since (cue tower blocks), but bohemian vibes live on at cafés and galleries. *{map 6}*

15th

Queuing for a table is rare in this sleepy district, given its lack of iconic sights. It may be quiet, but its foodie scene speaks volumes, and it's full of hidden gems. *{map 6}*

16th

Only the wealthiest Parisians can afford to live here, but everyone dreams about being able to. It's no wonder, considering the swanky 16th stretches along the Seine and brims with renowned museums. *{map 6}*

17th

Thanks to the hip Batignolles district, the 17th is shaking off its elite rep. It's a magnet for designers with its trendy bars and boutiques. *{map 4}*

18th

The 18th is often defined by arty Montmartre, but the Goutte d'Or – or Little Africa – is where it's at. A large African community have shaped this area, loved for its North African food trucks and Nigerian salons. *{map 4}*

19th

You know you're in the 19th when you can see green for days. Paris's two largest parks lie here, where families picnic and retirees play *pétanque*. *{map 5}*

20th

Free spirits have long been attracted to multicultural Belleville and Ménilmontant. While artists toil away in galleries, hipsters live it up in edgy bars. *{map 5}*

Paris
ON THE MAP

Whether you're looking for your
new favourite spot or want to check
out what each part of Paris has
to offer, our maps – along with
handy map references throughout
the book – have you covered.

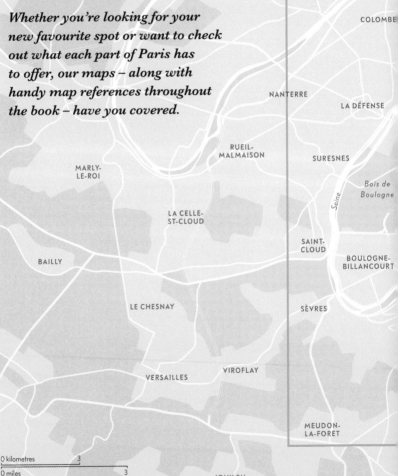

6

ARGENTEUIL

Seine

BEZONS

COLOMBE

NANTERRE

LA DÉFENSE

RUEIL-
MALMAISON

SURESNES

MARLY-
LE-ROI

Bois de
Boulogne

Seine

LA CELLE-
ST-CLOUD

SAINT-
CLOUD

BOULOGNE-
BILLANCOURT

BAILLY

LE CHESNAY

SÈVRES

VIROFLAY

VERSAILLES

MEUDON-
LA-FORET

0 kilometres   3

0 miles   3

JOUY-EN-
JOSAS

MAP 1

1

RUE RÉAUMUR

Rue Montorgueil

Bo&Mie **E**

Reset **N**   **A**
Musée de
l'Illusion

RUE RAMBUTEAU

Forum
s Halles

DE SÉBASTOPOL

PLACE J.
DU BELLAY

Le Labo
N

BOULEVARD

Théâtre
du Châtelet

QUAI DE GESVRES

Pont
Notre-Dame

ACE L.
PINE

RUE DE LA CITÉ

Île de
la Cité

Petit
Pont

Square
Jean XXIII

LATIN
QUARTER

5TH

RUE MONGE

Square
P Langevin

E EAT

Aki Boulangerie *(p33)*
Bo&Mie *(p34)*
Bouillon Racine *(p47)*
L'Abattoir Végétal *(p50)*

D DRINK

Freddy's *(p62)*
Treize au Jardin *(p59)*

S SHOP

E. Dehillerin *(p82)*
Kiliwatch *(p98)*
Librairie Galignani *(p92)*
Librairie Jousseaume *(p93)*
L'Officine Universelle Buly *(p103)*
Mad Lords *(p99)*
Nose *(p102)*
Oh My Cream! *(p101)*
The Red Wheelbarrow *(p95)*
Rouje *(p98)*
Shinzo *(p96)*

A ARTS & CULTURE

59 Rivoli *(p112)*
Museé de l'Illusion *(p118)*
Museé du Louvre *(p110)*

Museé du Luxembourg *(p108)*
Museé d'Orsay *(p109)*
Théâtre du Châtelet *(p123)*

N NIGHTLIFE

Église St Sulpice *(p143)*
Jardin du Carrousel *(p151)*
Jardin Nelson Mandela *(p151)*
Le Dernier Bar avant la
     Fin du Monde *(p147)*
Le Labo *(p152)*
Pont des Arts *(p150)*
Reset *(p145)*

O OUTDOORS

Galerie Vivienne *(p176)*
Jardin du Luxembourg *(p162)*
Jardin du Palais Royal *(p160)*
Marne River *(p171)*
Place Dauphine *(p179)*
Rue Montorgueil *(p177)*
Square du Vert-Galant *(p173)*

MAP 2

2

11TH

Merci

Maison Plisson

BOULEVARD BEAUMARCHAIS

BOULEVARD RICHARD LENOIR

BOULEVARD VOLTAIRE

Yellow Tucan

PLACE DE LA BASTILLE

BASTILLE

BOULEVARD BOURDON

Bassin de l'Arsenal

BOULEVARD DE LA BASTILLE

12TH

Ⓔ EAT

Au P'tit Grec *(p39)*

Baieta *(p46)*

Bar à Iode Saint Germain *(p45)*

Chez Alain Miam Miam *(p38)*

Elmer *(p46)*

Sacha Finkelsztajn *(p32)*

Ⓓ DRINK

Bisou *(p64)*

Caféothèque *(p59)*

Comptoir des Archives *(p73)*

La Belle Hortense *(p60)*

Lavomatic *(p67)*

Le Progrès *(p72)*

Les Philosophes Café *(p74)*

Little Red Door *(p65)*

Vignerons Parisiens *(p71)*

Yellow Tucan *(p56)*

Ⓢ SHOP

A la Ville de Rodez *(p83)*

CSAO *(p90)*

Faguo *(p97)*

Fleux *(p89)*

Huygens *(p101)*

Liquides Bar à Parfum *(p100)*

Maison Plisson *(p81)*

Merci *(p90)*

Papier Plus *(p92)*

Papier Tigre *(p94)*

Présence Africaine *(p93)*

Village Saint-Paul *(p86)*

Ⓐ ARTS & CULTURE

Black Paris Walks, le Paris Noir *(p126)*

Centre Pompidou *(p108)*

Ciné le Grand Action *(p120)*

Galerie Perrotin *(p112)*

Institut du Monde Arab *(p125)*

La Mutinerie *(p131)*

Maison Européenne de la Photographie *(p115)*

Musée d'Art et d'Histoire du Judaïsme *(p124)*

Musée des Arts et Métiers *(p111)*

Musée Carnavalet *(p124)*

Musée de Cluny *(p119)*

Panthéon *(p126)*

Rocky Horror at Studio Galande *(p121)*

Théâtre de la Ville de Paris *(p123)*

Ⓝ NIGHTLIFE

Jardin Tino-Rossi *(p150)*

Le Petit Fer á Cheval *(p154)*

Péniche Marcounet *(p137)*

Place du Marché Sainte-Catherine *(p149)*

Ⓞ OUTDOORS

Place Louis Aragon *(p163)*

Place des Vosges *(p163)*

Rue des Barres *(p177)*

PLACE DE LA
RÉPUBLIQUE

BOULEVARD RICHARD LENOIR

BOULEVARD DU TEMPLE

BOULEVARD VOLTAIRE

RUE JEAN-PIERRE TIMBAUD

Café
Chilango **E**

Utopie **E**

The Naked
Shop **S**

Le Bar à
Pintes **N**

La Place
Verte **N**

AVENUE DE

RUE

OBERKAMPF

RUE DE MÉNILMONTANT

Musée
Edith Piaf **A**

Chez
Bouboule **N**

Le Perchoir
Ménilmontant **N**

La Fine **D**
Mousse

BOULEVARD DE MÉNILMONTANT

Gossima **N**
Ping Pong
Bar

LA

RÉPUBLIQUE

11TH

Les Mots à
la Bouche **S**

Dirty Lemon **D**

Mr Alphonse **D**

Atelier des
Lumières **A**

RUE DU CHEMIN VERT

3RD

BLVD DES FILLES DU CALVAIRE

RUE DE TURENNE

BOULEVARD BEAUMARCHAIS

BOULEVARD RICHARD LENOIR

RUE LENOIR

BOULEVARD

CHEMIN

VERT

RUE DU CHEMIN

RUE ST-MAUR

Café du
Coin **N**

VOLTAIRE

PLACE
LÉON
BLUM

CheZaline **E**

VG Patisserie **E**

RUE LÉON FROT

Place des
Vosges

Back in Black **D**

RUE DE LA ROQUETTE

Lady
Long Solo **D**

AVENUE LEDRU-ROLLIN

BOULEVARD VOLTAIRE

Waly Fay **E**

RUE ST-ANTOINE

4TH

BLVD HENRI IV

PLACE
DE LA
BASTILLE

BASTILLE

RUE DU FAUBOURG ST-ANTOINE

Pizza Julia **E**

Le Chalet **E**
Savoyard

RUE DE CHARONNE

Mokoloco **E**

Les Cuves
de Fauve

11TH

RUE FAIDHERBE

Bistrot **E**
Paul Bert

Ailleurs **S**

Bassin de
l'Arsenal

BOULEVARD BOURDON

Bassin de l'Arsenal

Supersonic **N**

Stroll the
Coulée Verte **O**

Cycle **O**
the Canal

BLVD DE LA BASTILLE

Agrology **N**

Boulangerie **E**
Bo

Confiture
Parisienne **S**

Gamelle **N**

RUE DU FAUBOURG ST-ANTOINE

Le Baron Rouge **D**
Marché d'Aligre **S**

PLACE
D'ALIGRE

12TH

RUE DE REUILLY

Parc Rives **O**
de Seine

AVENUE LEDRU-ROLLIN

RUE DE LYON

RUE DE CHARENTON

AVENUE

BOULEVARD

DIDER

La Seine

BOULEVARD DIDEROT

DAUMESNIL

MAP 3

20TH

3

AVENUE GAMBETTA

⊙
Hike through
Cimetière du
Père Lachaise

AVENUE PHILIPPE AUGUSTE

Ⓔ Fulgurances
"l'Adresse"

BOULEVARD VOLTAIRE

RUE LÉON FROT

Ⓔ EAT

Bistrot Paul Bert *(p41)*
Boulangerie Bo *(p32)*
Café Chilango *(p42)*
CheZaline *(p36)*
Fulgurances "l'Adresse" *(p45)*
Le Chalet Savoyard *(p40)*
Mokoloco *(p38)*
Pizza Julia *(p49)*
Utopie *(p35)*
VG Patisserie *(p35)*
Waly Fay *(p41)*

Ⓓ DRINK

Back in Black *(p57)*
Dirty Lemon *(p65)*
La Fine Mousse *(p70)*
La Place Verte *(p75)*
Le Baron Rouge *(p62)*
Les Cuves de Fauve *(p68)*
Mr Alphonse *(p62)*

Ⓢ SHOP

Ailleurs *(p90)*
Confiture Parisienne *(p80)*
Lady Long Solo *(p95)*

Les Mots à la Bouche *(p94)*
Marché d'Aligre *(p84)*
The Naked Shop *(p102)*

Ⓐ ARTS & CULTURE

Atelier des Lumières *(p114)*
Musée Edith Piaf *(p118)*

Ⓝ NIGHTLIFE

Agrology *(p152)*
Café du Coin *(p153)*
Chez Bouboule *(p144)*
Gamelle *(p146)*
Gossima Ping Pong Bar *(p146)*
Le Bar à Pintes *(p145)*
Le Perchoir Ménilmontant *(p136)*
Supersonic *(p141)*

Ⓞ OUTDOORS

Bassin de l'Arsenal *(p169)*
Cycle the Canal *(p164)*
Hike through Cimetière du
    Père Lachaise *(p167)*
Parc Rives de Seine *(p168)*
Stroll the Coulée Verte *(p165)*

0 metres   300
0 yards   300

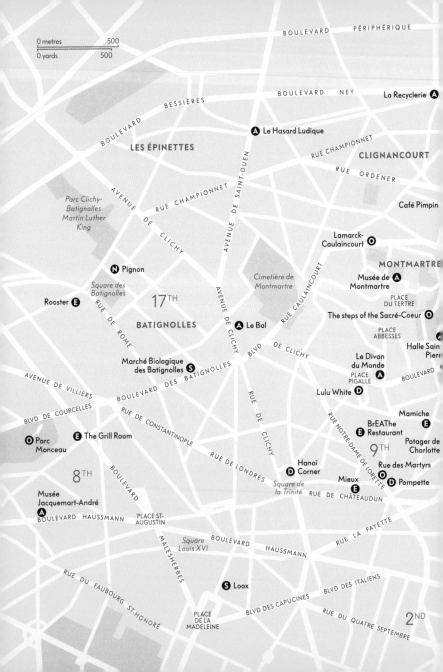

BOULEVARD PÉRIPHÉRIQUE

0 metres 500
0 yards 500

BOULEVARD NEY

La Recyclerie **A**

BESSIÈRES

A Le Hasard Ludique

LES ÉPINETTES

RUE CHAMPIONNET

CLIGNANCOURT

RUE ORDENER

Parc Clichy-
Batignolles
Martin Luther
King

AVENUE DE SAINT-OUEN

Café Pimpin

RUE CHAMPIONNET

AVENUE DE CLICHY

Lamarck-
Caulaincourt **D**

MONTMARTRE

N Pignon

Cimetière de
Montmartre

Musée de **A**
Montmartre

Square des
Batignolles

PLACE
DU TERTRE

17TH

RUE CAULAINCOURT

Rooster **E**

AVENUE DE CLICHY

The steps of the Sacré-Coeur **D**

RUE DE ROME

BATIGNOLLES

PLACE
ABBESSES

A Le Bal

Halle Saint
Pierre

Marché Biologique
des Batignolles **S**

BLVD DE CLICHY

Le Divan
du Monde

BOULEVARD DES BATIGNOLLES

PLACE
PIGALLE **A**

BOULEVARD

AVENUE DE VILLIERS

Lulu White **D**

BLVD DE COURCELLES

RUE DE CONSTANTINOPLE

RUE DE CLICHY

Mamiche **E**

BrEAThe **E**
Restaurant

D Parc
Monceau

E The Grill Room

RUE NOTRE-DAME-DE-LORETTE

9TH

Potager de
Charlotte

RUE DE LONDRES

Hanoï
Corner **D**

Rue des Martyrs **D**

8TH

BOULEVARD

Square de
la Trinité

Mieux
E

D Pompette

Musée
Jacquemart-André

RUE DE CHATEAUDUN

A
BOULEVARD HAUSSMANN

PLACE ST-
AUGUSTIN

MALESHERBES

Square
Louis XVI

BOULEVARD HAUSSMANN

RUE LA FAYETTE

RUE DU FAUBOURG ST-HONORE

S Loox

BLVD DES ITALIENS

PLACE
DE LA
MADELEINE

BLVD DES CAPUCINES

RUE DU QUATRE SEPTEMBRE

2ND

MAP 4

4

ⒺEAT

BrEAThe Restaurant (p50)

The Grill Room (p47)

Jah Jah by le Tricycle (p48)

Mamiche (p35)

Mieux (p44)

Potager de Charlotte (p51)

Rooster (p46)

ⒹDRINK

Brasserie de la
    Goutte d'Or (p68)

Café Pimpin (p59)

Dev!ant (p61)

Hanoï Corner (p57)

Lulu White (p67)

Pompette (p61)

⒮SHOP

Isakin (p99)

Le Vin au Vert (p81)

Loox (p103)

Marché Biologique
    des Batignolles (p87)

Marché Dejean (p87)

Marché Saint-Pierre (p85)

ⒶARTS & CULTURE

Halle Saint-Pierre (p113)

La Recyclerie (p128)

Le Bal (p113)

Le Divan du Monde (p121)

Le Hasard Ludique (p131)

Le Louxor (p123)

Musée Jacquemart-André (p117)

Musée de Montmartre (p119)

⒩NIGHTLIFE

Pignon (p153)

⒪OUTDOORS

Lamarck-Caulaincourt (p174)

Parc Monceau (p161)

Rue des Martyrs (p178)

The steps of the Sacré-Coeur (p172)

0 metres 500
0 yards 500

BOULEVARD NEY

LA CHAPELLE

RUE DE LA CHAPELLE

RUE DE L'EVANGILE

RUE D'AUBERVILLIERS

RUE DE CRIMÉE

La Gare

À La Folie Paris

19TH

18TH

RUE ORDENER

RUE RIQUET

Le Shakirail

104 Centquatre

LA VILLETTE

L'Eau et les Rêves

AVENUE DE FLANDRE

Bassin de la Villette

Paname Brewing Company

RUE MARX DORMOY

Les Jardins d'Éole

Bassin de la Villette

Quai de la Loire

BOULEVARD DE LA CHAPELLE

La Rotonde Stalingrad

PLACE DE LA BATAILLE DE STALINGRAD

AVENUE JEAN JAURÈS

RUE ARMAND CARREL

RUE MANIN

Parc des Buttes-Chaumont

Rosa Bonhe

RUE DE CRI

RUE BOTZARIS

19TH

BOULEVARD DE MAGENTA

RUE DU FAUBOURG ST-DENIS

RUE LA FAYETTE

RUE DU FAUBOURG ST-MARTIN

Le Top du Point Ephémère

New Soul Food

Canal Saint-Martin

PLACE DU COL. FABIEN

AVENUE SIMÓN BOLÍVAR

Pavillon Puebla

BOULEVARD DE LA VILLETTE

10TH

La Fontaine

La Sardine

Le Cadoret

BELLEVILLE

BMK

Urfa Dürüm

Taka & Vermo

Velan

Passage Brady

 Sergeant Paper

Marché Saint-Martin

La Trésorerie

BLVD DE STRASBOURG

BLVD DE MAGENTA

Less is More

Early June

Passerelle Richerand

Chez Prune

Gros Bao

Tien Hiang

La Marine

Canal Saint-Martin

RUE DU FAUBOURG DU TEMPLE

Le Pacifique

Cantine Primeur

Parc de Belleville

La Commune

BOULEVARD DE BELLEVILLE

BLVD DE SÉBASTOPOL

RUE ST-MARTIN

BLVD ST-MARTIN

PLACE DE LA RÉPUBLIQUE

11TH

MAP 5

5

Parc de
la Villette

néma en Ⓐ
Plein Air   Ⓝ
Philharmonie
de Paris

JEAN   JAURÈS

RUE MANIN

Ⓒ Café
Chéri(e)   PLACE DES
FÊTES

UE   DE   BELLEVILLE

RUE DES PYRÉNÉES

20TH

MÉNILMONTANT

Ⓝ
La Bellevilloise

Ⓔ EAT

Cantine Primeur *(p48)*

Early June *(p40)*

Gros Bao *(p39)*

Le Cadoret *(p42)*

Le Pacifique *(p42)*

New Soul Food *(p37)*

Tien Hiang *(p49)*

Urfa Dürüm *(p37)*

Ⓓ DRINK

Café Chéri(e) *(p64)*

Chez Prune *(p56)*

La Commune *(p67)*

La Marine *(p74)*

La Rotonde Stalingrad *(p75)*

La Sardine *(p72)*

Paname Brewing Company *(p70)*

Ⓢ SHOP

BMK *(p82)*

La Trésorerie *(p89)*

L'Eau et les Rêves *(p95)*

Less is More *(p97)*

Marché Saint-Martin *(p85)*

Sergeant Paper *(p88)*

Taka & Vermo *(p81)*

Velan *(p82)*

Ⓐ ARTS & CULTURE

104 Centquatre *(p128)*

Cinéma en Plein Air *(p120)*

Le Shakirail *(p129)*

Ⓝ NIGHTLIFE

À La Folie Paris *(p146)*

Canal Saint-Martin *(p148)*

La Bellevilloise *(p140)*

La Fontaine *(p154)*

La Gare *(p142)*

Le Top du Point Ephémère *(p139)*

Pavillon Puebla *(p139)*

Philharmonie de Paris *(p143)*

Quai de la Loire *(p148)*

Rosa Bonheur *(p136)*

Ⓞ OUTDOORS

Bassin de la Villette *(p169)*

Parc de Belleville *(p174)*

Parc des Buttes-Chaumont *(p160)*

Passage Brady *(p178)*

Passerelle Richerand *(p173)*

ARGENTEUIL

SAINT-DENIS

La Seine

BEZONS

GENNEVILLIERS

COLOMBES

ASNIÈRES-
SUR-SEINE

La Seine

AUBERVILLIER

CLICHY

BLVD PÉRIPHÉRIQUE

LA DÉFENSE

NEUILLY-
SUR-SEINE 17TH

Fondation
Louis Vuitton Ⓐ

*See maps 1–5
for Central Paris*

SURESNES

Ⓞ

Palais
Galliera

Ⓓ La Vigne de
Suresnes

Jog the Bois de
Boulogne

Marché Ⓐ
Président-Wilson Ⓢ Ⓐ Palais de Tokyo

La Seine

Cité de l'Architecture Ⓐ Ⓐ Musée du Quai
et du Patrimoine Branly–Jacques Chirac

PASSY

Pont de Ⓞ
Bir-Hakeim

Ⓐ
Musée Rodin

Cravan Ⓝ

Ⓐ
Parc du
Champ-
de-Mars

Ⓐ
Musée
Rodin

SAINT-
CLOUD

16TH

Piscine Molitor Ⓞ

Ⓝ
Bowling de
Paris Front de Seine

15TH

Le
Mazette

Grou
Cont

Ⓝ

Ⓐ

BOULOGNE-
BILLANCOURT

Ride the Ballon
de Paris Generali

Ⓞ

Skate with Ⓢ
Pari Roller

MONTPARNASSE

Grande Mosquée Ⓓ
de Paris

Parc d
Berc

Ⓞ
Parc de
Saint-Cloud

Ⓝ La Seine
Musicale

ISSY-LES-
MOULINEAUX

Find the Petite
Ceinture

Ⓞ

14TH

Ⓐ
Fondation
Cartier pour l'Art
Contemporain

Piscine
Joséphine Baker

Ⓞ Ⓞ

Ⓔ
Season Square

Quai François Mauriac

La Jave

SÈVRES

Ⓢ
Marché aux Puces
de la Porte de Vanves

Ⓞ
Butte-aux-
Cailles

13TH

BLVD PÉRIPHÉRIQUE

MONTROUGE

IVRY-SUR-
SEINE

ARCUEIL

CLAMART

BAGNEUX

VILLEJUIF

0 kilometres   2

0 miles   2

SCEAUX

MAP 6

6

🄴 EAT

Benoît Castel (p34)

Season Square (p50)

🄳 DRINK

Bar Gallia (p71)

Grand Mosquée de Paris (p73)

La Vigne de Suresnes (p69)

🅂 SHOP

Marché Président-Wilson (p84)

Marché aux Puces de la
Porte de Vanves (p86)

🄰 ARTS & CULTURE

Cité de l'Architecture et du
Patrimoine (p109)

Fondation Cartier pour l'Art
Contemporain (p115)

Fondation Louis Vuitton (p114)

Ground Control (p131)

Musée des Arts Forains (p117)

Musée Nationale de l'Histoire
de l'Immigration (p127)

Musée du Quai Branly–
Jacques Chirac (p116)

Musée Rodin (p127)

Palais Galliera (p111)

Palais de Tokyo (p110)

🄽 NIGHTLIFE

Bowling de Paris Front
de Seine (p147)

Cirque Électrique (p142)

Cravan (p154)

La Javelle (p139)

La Seine Musicale (p140)

Le Mazette (p141)

Mama Shelter East (p137)

Parc du Champ-de-Mars (p149)

🄾 OUTDOORS

Bois de Vincennes (p163)

Butte-aux-Cailles (p176)

Find the Petite Ceinture (p166)

Jog the Bois de Boulogne (p166)

La Campagne à Paris (p178)

Parc de Bercy (p162)

Parc de Saint-Cloud (p172)

Piscine Joséphine Baker (p171)

Piscine Molitor (p168)

Pont de Bir-Hakeim (p174)

Quai François Mauriac (p171)

Ride the Ballon de Paris
Generali (p165)

Sand Fabrik (p164)

Skate with Pari Roller (p167)

🄾 Sand Fabrik

PANTIN

🄳 Bar Gallia

🄽 Cirque
Électrique

🄴 Benoît Castel

🄾 La Campagne
à Paris

🄽 Mama
Shelter East

20ᵀᴴ

VINCENNES

Musée Nationale
de l'Histoire de
l'Immigration

2ᵀᴴ 🄰

usée des
rts Forains

🄾 Bois de
Vincennes

La Seine

VITRY-SUR-
SEINE

EAT

Food is the soul of Paris. Good cooking and good company are held sacred in time-honoured brasseries, bistros with a modern edge and laidback dining rooms.

Perfect Patisseries

Nothing defines Paris quite like the patisserie. While it's a myth that Parisians eat croissants every morning, bread is bought freshly baked daily, and picking up a tart is more sophisticated than making your own.

SACHA FINKELSZTAJN

Map 2; 27 Rue des Rosiers, 4th; ///smirks.barmaid.debate; www.laboutiquejaune.fr

Boutique Jaune, as it's commonly known thanks to its *jaune* (yellow) façade, is the most traditional of the Yiddish bakeries in the heart of Paris's Jewish community. It's been family run for three generations and is delightfully old school: queue once to browse the breads and bagels, then again to pay with a paper ticket at the till. Shopping here has changed little since opening in 1946, only adding to its charm.

BOULANGERIE BO

Map 3; 85 bis Rue de Charenton, 12th; ///confined.fault.skews; 01 43 07 75 21

Imagine a watercolour painting of an archetypal French bakery – on the corner of a Haussmannian building, with picture windows and gold signage – and you've got Boulangerie Bo. The inventive patisserie creations are just as beautiful as the shop's surrounds, in the sleepy side streets near the Marché d'Aligre *(p84)*. Customer favourites are the gorgeous strawberry tarts with a veil of cucumber gel and the delicate raspberry hibiscus meringues.

AKI BOULANGERIE

Map 1; 16 Rue Sainte-Anne, 1st; ///bottle.archive.orbit; www.akiboulanger.com

Surrounded by Japanese restaurants that draw crowds at night, Aki's popularity peaks during the day. By all appearances just another Parisian bakery, it's lined with cases filled with matcha-infused favourites and classics like éclairs and mille feuilles. French pastry never really gets boring, but Aki offers a unique mash-up that you won't find anywhere else in the city – or likely the world.

» Don't leave without trying the iced matcha latte – it's not sugary like it is in Japan, so pairs well with any of the cakes.

Shh!

Okay, we know: Legay Choc, with its bright-pink exterior and rainbow-striped awning, isn't *really* that under the radar *(www.legaychoc.fr)*. But how could we miss it off the list? It claims to be Paris's first gay bakery, after all. Run by two brothers, who's surname just happens to be Legay, this cheeky spot is famous for its rather risqué baguettes and brioches, which come in the shape of, ahem, the family jewels.

BO&MIE

Map 1; 18 Rue de Turbigo, 2nd; ///dance.broads.dunes; www.boetmie.com

Don't expect a classic boulangerie experience here: this creative spot is on a mission to reimagine French baking traditions. That doesn't mean compromising on quality or technique, but rather having fun with flavours. Plan to have a BFF catch-up here in the morning with a praliné *pain au chocolat*, and you'll probably still be here chatting away in the afternoon over a lemon-lime madeleine.

BENOÎT CASTEL

Map 6; 150 Rue de Ménilmontant, 20th;
///familiar.quarrel.roses; www.benoitcastel.com

Any Ménilmontant local will tell you this boulangerie changed their life. Named after the pastry chef at its helm, this homely spot exudes a strong community spirit, where cheerful staff work in the open kitchen. It's at the top of one of Paris's steepest streets, so once you've made the climb, have a well-deserved signature tart – the recipes of which honour Castel's Brittany roots.

Try it!
MASTER THE MACARON

Making a signature macaron is as tricky as you might expect, but you can have fun trying with Cook'n With Class *(www.cooknwithclass.com/paris)*. It runs three-hour classes so you can learn the secrets.

UTOPIE

Map 3; 20 Rue Jean-Pierre Timbaud, 11th; ///heap.outlines.paving; 09 82 50 74 48

There's always a line out the door at this modern corner patisserie and boulangerie, where the tantalizing aroma of fresh croissants emerging from the ovens will have you scheming ways to jump the queue. Just remember to grab a *pain au chocolat* when get to the front; they disappear into paper bags quicker than the chefs can bake them.

» Don't leave without trying the black *charbon végétal* baguette made with activated charcoal – it'll look great in your picnic pictures.

VG PATISSERIE

Map 3; 123 Rue Voltaire; ///visa.monopoly.wounds; www.vgpatisserie.fr

Take dairy away from French patisserie and there's not much left. Enter Bérénice Leconte, the queen of Parisian vegan pastry. Creamy mousse cake, soft croissants and seasonal crispy tartlets are made with her flawless craftsmanship and organic ingredients to fool your taste buds (and wallet – they're surprisingly affordable).

MAMICHE

Map 4; 45 Rue Condorcet, 9th; ///grading.repeated.masters; www.mamiche.fr

Run by a young team, this neighbourhood bakery is taking Paris by storm with an unpretentious approach to great baking. You won't find elaborate tarts or fussy macaron flavours here, but rather pillowy orange-flower brioche, gooey brownies and perfectly baked baguettes.

Lunch on the Go

It's a fact: Parisians are big fans of a decadent sit-down lunch. On days when time just doesn't allow, however, locals love nothing more than picking up a light bite and eating al fresco in a park or along the riverbank.

CHEZALINE

Map 3; 85 Rue de la Roquette, 11th; ///quench.tomorrow.january; 01 43 71 90 75

If you worship at the altar of crusty bread and salty butter, this is your place of pilgrimage. For nearly a decade, this tiny café-deli has been the go-to sandwich spot for all manner of locals. Once a horse-meat butcher (the "Z" in CheZaline replaces the "v" of *boucherie chevaline*), the shop is still delightfully retro and there's an

Try it!
MAKE A SANDWICH

The Prince de Paris ham that's generously stuffed into sandwiches at CheZaline is considered France's finest, so pick some up from A la Ville de Rodez *(p83)* to make your own treat.

old-school vibe to the proceedings, where sandwiches are wrapped in butcher paper. It's a tiny space, so tuck into your liberally buttered ham baguette as you stroll to the Bassin de l'Arsenal *(p169)*.

NEW SOUL FOOD

Map 5; 177 Quai de Valmy, 10th; ///eagles.combines.porch; www.newsoulfood.fr

This restaurant and its additional roving food truck are spreading street-food-style dining across Paris – an exciting concept in a city where sit-down meals are sacred. Mixing culinary influences from across Africa and the Caribbean, New Soul Food is big on flavour and low on formality. You'll have to check its social pages to find the food-truck schedule, and the menu changes by day, but this is all part of the fun and why it's quickly built a large fanbase.

URFA DÜRÜM

Map 5; 58 Rue du Faubourg Saint-Denis, 10th; ///kite.bronzes.gosh

Any sandwich-loving Parisian will tell you this hole-in-the-wall Kurdish joint – set amid the chaos of discount clothing stores, bijou coffee shops and traditional butchers – is a must-visit. Despite lacking an online presence, Urfa Dürüm has a cult following thanks to the office workers who pop by for the amazing flatbreads (made as you watch) and persuade their colleagues to join them the next day. Taking in the hubbub of the adjoining street is all part of the joy of waiting.

» Don't leave without trying the incredible lamb-filled *dürüm*, the meat smoky from the grill and wrapped tightly with fresh salad.

MOKOLOCO

Map 3; 74 Rue de Charonne, 11th; ///timidly.hosts.grants;
www.mokoloco.fr

You'd be hard-pressed to find anyone who lives in the 11th that
hasn't fallen in love with Mokoloco's unique flavours. This isn't your
average sandwich spot: as at nearby sibling café Mokonuts, owners
Moko Hirayama and Omar Koreitem have created a fun, fresh and
one-of-a-kind menu that blends Middle Eastern, American, and
Japanese flavours and ingredients. Thanks to a large and devoted
fanbase, you'll need to wait in line at lunch, when it's at its busiest –
but the reward for missing half your lunch break are unreal katsu
brioche buns and sloppy joes. It's a real *coup de coeur* (something
special), as the French say.

» Don't leave without trying Moko's famous chocolate and oatmeal
cookies. They're baked to order and come warm, soft and chewy.

CHEZ ALAIN MIAM MIAM

Map 2; Marché des Enfants Rouges, 3rd;
///fuss.exams.spot; 09 86 17 28 00

It's easy to see why the inimitable Alain has one of the longest-running
stalls in the Marché des Enfants Rouges, the oldest market in Paris.
First: his distinctive take on the humble sandwich. Second: his
charisma – a song or dance while he whips up your lunch is pretty
commonplace. As you amble through the market, you'll know you've
found the right stall when you spot Alain on the *biligs* (the round
cast-iron stovetops on which crêpes are sizzled), preparing food for
the longest queue. Tourists come for the enormous buckwheat

If you'd prefer to tackle hot pancakes with a knife and fork, head to Alain's nearby sit-down spot at 26 Rue Charlot.

galettes, but those in the know order his sandwiches and *socca* (chickpea pancakes). All are impractical to eat, but that's just part of the fun. *Miam miam!*

AU P'TIT GREC

Map 2; 68 Rue Mouffetard, 5th; ///respect.jeep.star; www.auptitgrec.com

Among the kitschy English menus of Rue Mouffetard, this place remains a local favourite, not least among students. If there's no line, count your blessings. The crêpes here are hearty, slightly sinful and far from elegant, with creative concoctions like l'Italien, topped by coppa and mozzarella, proving a big hit. Grab a couple of extra napkins (you're going to need them for these oozing crêpes) and perch up in the nearby Arènes de Lutèce.

GROS BAO

Map 5; 72 Quai de Jemmapes, 10th; ///assure.graced.scouted;
www.baofamily.co/grosbao

Red is seen as a lucky colour in China, so perhaps that's why this trendy Chinese restaurant, set on the Canal Saint-Martin, is doused in the colour. The lamps are red, the floor is red and the walls – well, you get it. You're going to need good fortune to grab a seat here, too: at lunch, crowds descend on this spot for the lip-smackingly delicious dishes (think fluffy char sui bao and spicy Sichuan-style mapo tofu). Luckily, they also do takeout, so you can grab some bao or black-pepper beef and find a place to gorge on the canal.

Cosy Dinners

A late, lazy dinner is the Parisian way. Make a reservation for 8pm at the absolute earliest, settle in for two courses and dessert, and let the awaited catch-ups commence between it all.

EARLY JUNE

Map 5; 19 Rue Jean Poulmarch, 10th;
///shopper.dare.blaring; www.early-june.fr

Eating at this cool bar-restaurant is like dining at a friend's home, where dishes are made one by one in the tiny kitchen and delivered to every table that orders at the same time. Reserve a candlelit table and settle in for the evening to swap news over sharing plates and orange wines. Set back from the canalside melee, Early June is missed by those who venture no further than the *quais*, so it's a nicely kept secret.

LE CHALET SAVOYARD

Map 3; 58 Rue de Charonne, 11th;
///bills.vine.juggle; www.chalet-savoyard.fr

Meals centred around melted cheese are Parisian essentials during the winter. If you've not yet purchased a raclette machine, this is where to come for a true taste of the Alps; here, tables are laden with pots

To throw your own raclette party, head to Fromagerie Beaufils in the 20th to pick up the cheeses in season. of tempting fondue, while enormous wheels of Morbier sizzle under table-top grills. It's a sociable feast, where cheese comas and good conversations linger.

WALY FAY

Map 3; 6 Rue Godefroy Cavaignac, 11th; ///trample.logic.squeaks; www.walyfay.fr

This isn't the kind of spot you only come to once. The benches inside this low-key restaurant are always filled with a regular clientele who return for the delicious Senegalese and other West African dishes that they rave about to their friends. Service is warm and relaxed, if decidedly leisurely in comparison to the usual Parisian pace, so it feels like a home away from home. Come hungry: whether you order fried plantain or grilled chicken, portions are enormous.

BISTROT PAUL BERT

Map 3; 18 Rue Paul Bert, 11th; ///dragons.held.suitcase; 01 43 72 24 01

Truly deserving of its many accolades, this is the perfect French bistro. From the tiled floors to the polished tables, it's all about tradition here. Owner Bertrand Auboyneau is a bit of a legend among the city's gourmands, but there's no pretention: expect a warm welcome and plenty of help deciphering the chalkboard menus.

›› Don't leave without trying one of the classic desserts, like the Grand Marnier soufflé. This oh-so-fluffy, liqueur-spiked masterpiece is as decadent as they come.

LE PACIFIQUE

Map 5; 35 Rue de Belleville, 19th; ///outfit.crystals.chew; 01 42 49 66 80

At this charming neighbourhood joint, loyal regulars cluster around traditional banquet tables laden with Cantonese-style dim sum and roast meats. As the smell of roast duck wafts through the room, pull up a chair and tuck into plate after plate of homemade dim sum.

LE CADORET

Map 5; 1 Rue Pradier, 19th; ///hounded.posed.smoothly; 01 53 21 92 13

With mosaic floors and mirror-backed banquettes, Le Cadoret may look traditional, but it's a subtle reinvention of a neighbourhood bistro for Belleville's increasingly "bobo" (bourgeois-bohemian) residents. The wine list is the highlight here: a who's who of pioneering natural winemakers that draws devotees from across Paris (much to the dismay of Belleville locals, who would rather keep this place a secret).

» Don't leave without trying the *tête de veau*. Okay, boiled calf's head doesn't sound delicious, but this rich dish is done so well here.

CAFÉ CHILANGO

Map 3; 82 Rue de la Folie Méricourt, 11th;
///restless.stapled.raves; www.cafechilangoparis.com

Banish visions of guacamole served with ready-salted crisps (it's more common here than you'd think): this Mexican-run spot is the real deal. With its brick walls and wooden floors, it's a warm and welcoming place – the kind where you can add a stool to the table when another friend turns up for margaritas and good vibes.

Liked by the locals

"In the bistro, there are rules.
Rosé is for an apéritif not dinner,
the chef's word is final and don't
even think about changing cutlery
between courses. But this – and
the cracked tile floors, the burnt
robusta and the pots of wine –
make me happy."

JESS TIMMINS, PARIS MANAGER AT DEVOUR TOURS

Top Formules

The great French tradition of the multi-course meal endures. Parisians flock to the latest "it" spots for affordable mid-week formules at lunch, while tasting menus are reserved for celebrations at the weekends.

MIEUX

Map 4; 21 Rue Saint-Lazare, 9th; ///asteroid.star.tricks;

www.mieux-restaurant.com

Run by friends, for friends, this trendy spot is one of the city's much-loved neo-bistros. The two-floor dining room gives off the vibe of an effortlessly cool apartment, particularly when candlelit without even

Shh!

Hidden inside Napoleon's imposing Église de la Madeleine is Le Foyer de la Madeleine (*www.foyerdelamadeleine.fr*), a galleried, not-for-profit lunchtime-only restaurant that's become a well-kept secret among office workers and students in the area. Expect to spend around €20 on a tasty three-course lunch including cheese and dessert, or half that if you purchase an annual membership. It's a steal.

a hint of a cliché at night. With a low-cost, three-course lunch *formule* (led by what produce is in that week), it's little wonder Mieux is popular with the start-up crowd who work in the "Silicon IX" nearby.

FULGURANCES "L'ADRESSE"

Map 3; 10 Rue Alexandre Dumas, 11th; ///finishes.struggle.student; wwww.fulgurances.com

You never know what will grace the menu at this one-of-a-kind spot, where rising stars are invited for residencies to hone their menus before branching out solo. This means exceptional-quality cooking for a fraction of what you'd pay in a Michelin-star dining room – and bragging rights that you've discovered the next big culinary trends. Plan to spend around €80 on a multi-course meal with wine at a treat-the-parents dinner.

BAR À IODE SAINT GERMAIN

Map 2; 34 Boulevard Saint-Germain, 5th; ///cone.original.mere; www.baraiode.fr

The no-frills approach to serving seafood straight from the Brittany and Normandy coasts is a breath of fresh (and salty) air here. This casual spot is a short stroll from the busiest part of the Boulevard, so you're unlikely to stumble upon it without a recommendation. Die-hard fans will tell you to head here at lunch for the bargain set menu, which is always seasonal and always delicious.

» Don't leave without trying a glass of Muscadet: the classic pairing with shellfish. If you find a bottle you like, you can buy it to take away.

ELMER

Map 2; 30 Rue Notre Dame de Nazareth, 3rd;
///cocktail.hung.stretch; www.elmer-restaurant.fr

Stylish "working" lunches and dinners with friends are the name of the game at this elegant restaurant, set on a road lined with classic white-shuttered apartments. The great-value *formule* (including a two-course set menu) is really set apart by the warm service, so you'll feel comfortable lingering here for hours while tucking into classic French food with a twist.

ROOSTER

Map 4; 137 Rue Cardinet, 17th; ///uproot.drove.zest;
www.rooster-restaurant.com

Frédéric Duca's Batignolles restaurant is reason alone to schlep to the 17th. Duca hails from Marseille and southern flavours shine on his bistronomy-style menu. You can rack up a serious bill if you choose the full tasting menu with wine pairings (essential) at dinner, so opt for the two-course lunch if you're not celebrating a special occasion.

BAIETA

Map 2; 5 Rue de Pontoise, 5th; ///outdone.nutrients.bring;
www.restaurant-baieta-paris.fr

In a city where the fine-dining scene remains dominated by men, a Michelin-starred restaurant from the country's youngest female chef is something to celebrate. Julia Sedefdjian's restaurant is as minimalist as they come, designed to amplify the flavours and beauty of her

Post-meal, visit Baieta's sister bar Bô around the corner to sample one of its 70 niche Caribbean rums.

Niçoise-influenced dishes. Splash out on the three-course lunch menu and you'll fall in love – the restaurant's name means "little kiss" in the Niçois dialect, after all.

BOUILLON RACINE

Map 1; 3 Rue Racine, 6th; ///zapped.chefs.pelted; www.bouillonracine.fr

One step inside Bouillon Racine and you'll feel like you've been transported back to Paris's belle époque period. The place is gloriously Art Nouveau, with elegant mirrored walls, an intricate mosaic floor, and wrought-iron chairs and chandeliers; in fact, the decor here is so stunning, this restaurant has been listed as a Historic Monument. Amazingly, despited the gilded glamour, the formules remain very resonably priced, costing just €35 for a multi-course dinner of classic French fare.

THE GRILL ROOM

Map 4; 73 Rue de Monceau, 8th;
///supplied.delved.trendy; 01 42 89 59 26

Brunch may not be the biggest deal in Paris, but this glitzy spot is leading a hollandaise-smothered revolution. The vibe here is chic but not stuffy, so dress up and head here on a Sunday for the set four-course brunch – plus a glass or two of bubbly, of course. It's the perfect place to catch up with friends.

» Don't leave without trying the *brioche perdu* – decadent "French" toast drizzled with a salted butter caramel sauce.

Veggie and Vegan

While some old-guard chefs still present vegetarians with chicken stock-spiked sauces and a shrug, meat-free cooking is on the rise, led by a generation of plant-based foodies and forward-thinking restaurants.

CANTINE PRIMEUR

Map 5; 4 Rue Lemon, 20th; ///revives.dreams.sugar; www.cantineprimeur.fr

You'd never guess that this lunchtime-only spot, with its conventional café-cantine façade, is a plant-based restaurant. It's a far cry from other vegan spots across central Paris, where style sometimes takes precedence over substance. Instead, the menu here speaks volumes: it's seasonal, but some dishes – the bo bun and three-veg lasagne – make regular appearances. Set on a quiet street back from traffic-choked Boulevard de Belleville, you need to know it's here to find it.

JAH JAH BY LE TRICYCLE

Map 4; 11 Rue des Petites Écuries, 10th; ///pints.rejected.amount; 01 46 27 38 03

It's rare to chat to your neighbours when you're out for a meal in Paris, but then it's also rare to find a canteen-style Rasta restaurant right in the centre of the city. Jah Jah bucks the rules and sets trends instead, attracting an enormously diverse clientele from office workers to students. The food is healthy in the sense that it's plant-based, but it's all about piling as much as possible on your table, whether that's huge vegan bowls or burgers accompanied by enormous salads.

PIZZA JULIA

**Map 3; 43 Rue de Charenton, 12th; ///ever.boasted.hardens;
www.pizzajulia.fr**

It's easy to walk past Pizza Julia's unassuming exterior and not give a thought to what lies behind – but this would be a mistake, believe us. Run by award-winning chef Gérard Giovanni, this little hole-in-the-wall pizzeria serves up the best vegan pizza in Paris (veggie and meat versions are offered, too). Local vegans descend here to devour slice after slice of The Prestige, where a shallot-and-squash creamed base is topped with things like grilled aubergines, artichokes and pine nuts.

>> Don't leave without admiring Gérard's awards (next to the ordering window), including one naming him world champion of vegan pizza.

TIEN HIANG

Map 5; 14 Rue Bichat, 10th; ///competent.probable.oval; www.tien-hiang.fr

This tiny, family-run spot has been a pioneer of vegan Asian food since the 1990s, thanks to its hallmark simple dishes with mesmerizing textures – all inspired by traditional Buddhist cuisine. The "beef", "chicken" and "shrimp" don't sacrifice on taste, so much so that Tien Hiang has become the favourite place for local vegans to convert their sceptical carnivore friends.

L'ABATTOIR VÉGÉTAL

Map 1; 9 Rue Guisarde, 6th; ///blend.condiment.deck;
www.abattoirvegetal.com

The first incarnation of this flower-filled vegan restaurant was located
in a disused abattoir – hence the slightly macabre name. It may have
since moved south of the Seine, but the food remains as delicious
as ever: think fruit-topped vegan pancakes and homemade granola
with non-dairy yogurt. All the dishes are made with seasonal, organic
ingredients and are eye-poppingly colourful; in fact, they're so pretty,
it'd be rude not to take a snap of them for your socials.

BREATHE RESTAURANT

Map 4; 16 Rue Henry Monnier, 9th; ///tanks.buzz.relaxing;
www.breathe-restaurant.com

You'll need to make a reservation at this trendy modern restaurant,
where even carnivores are clamouring to taste the seitan burgers. If
your veggie pal is in town at the weekend, skip the classic meals and
book for the "tea time" instead to impress them with handmade cakes.
Everything is specially designed with coeliacs in mind, too.

SEASON SQUARE

Map 6; 3 Rue Louise Weiss, 13th; ///fencing.luggage.asleep;
www.season-square.com

Don't let the massive concrete pillar at the entrance deter you: Season
Square may not look like much, but trust the local devotees when
they say this is where you'll find the best vegan burger. The fluffy

bun, juicy veggie steak and savvy sauce combination create an elegantly balanced taste. Most of the customers are from the office district nearby, but true vegan gourmets cross the Seine for a taste of the healthy, homemade seasonal cuisine here.

» Don't leave without trying the cinnamon roll, if you're lucky and there's any left. The flavoursome doughy bread is unbeatable.

POTAGER DE CHARLOTTE

Map 4; 12 Rue Louise-Émilie de la Tour d'Auvergne, 9th;
///unstable.dream.campers; www.lepotagerdecharlotte.fr

When it comes to vegan fine dining (once unthinkable in Paris), banish any ideas you have about meat substitutes or meat-free imitations of classic dishes. Instead, fresh and seasonal cooking reigns supreme in this swish, royal-green dining room. Combinations that sound simple – such as grilled courgettes with a tomato sauce, rice and pesto – are anything but in flavour and appearance. Two brothers are responsible for this kitchen magic, where plates are as colourful and photo-worthy as in any contemporary bistro.

Try it!
PICK UP PLANT-BASED

For ingredients to whip up your own meat-free meal, check out the vegan concept store Aujourd'hui Demain *(42 Rue du Chemin Vert, 11th)*. It stocks vegan clothing and beauty products, too.

BASTILLE

RUE DU FAUBOURG ST-ANTOINE

AVENUE LEDRU ROLLIN

11TH

Indulge in a long lunch at
BISTROT PAUL BERT

This old-school bistro is as
quintessentially Parisian as it
gets. Order the *steak-frites* —
they're the best in the city.

4

RUE P. BERT

FAUBOURG
ST-ANTOINE

Raise a glass at
LE BARON ROUGE

A pre-noon glass of wine is a
Parisian staple. Embrace it
and sip a beautiful Burgundy
at this market-trader haunt.

RUE DU FAUBOURG ST-ANTOINE

PLACE
MIREILLE
HAVET

RUE DE COTTE

RU CROZATIER

3

1

RUE E. CASTELAR

2

Amble through
MARCHÉ D'ALIGRE

Squeeze your way through
the tightly packed stalls of this
market, traders shouting as
they vie for your attention.

Fuel up at
BOULANGERIE BO

Start your day with a
Parisian essential from this
picture-perfect boulangerie:
a croissant still delightfully
warm from the oven.

RUE DE CHARENTON

VIADUC DES ARTS

BOULEVARD DIDEROT

RUE CHALIGNY

12TH

*Many artisans make up
the* **Viaduc des Arts**
*community, where a
series of gourmet havens
lie beneath former
railway arches.*

PLACE DU
COLONEL
BOURGOIN

5

Get artistic at
ATELIER C

Paris takes its chocolate
seriously. Do the same
and try your hand at a
chocolate-making class,
held in this concept-
store-meets-workshop.

AVENUE DAUMESNIL

BERCY

0 metres   250
0 yards   250

A morning of
food in the 12th

Parisian food culture is centred on great ingredients — shopping isn't a weekly chore, but a daily joy. In addition to independent fromageries and butchers, every arrondissement has at least one fresh produce market, where stalls are laden with seasonal fruit and vegetables. The Marché d'Aligre is one of the few to open six days a week, and supplies the restaurants nearby with fresh produce and inspiration. There's no more exciting place to be than the 12th, filling tote bags with groceries and dipping into time-honoured haunts.

1. Boulangerie Bo
85 bis Rue de
Charenton, 12th;
01 43 07 75 21
///confined.fault.skews

2. Marché d'Aligre
Place d'Aligre, 12th; www.
marchedaligre.free.fr
///coveted.qualified.readings

3. Le Baron Rouge
1 Rue Théophile Roussel,
12th; www.lebaronrouge.net
///marker.risen.possibly

4. Bistrot Paul Bert
18 Rue Paul Bert, 11th;
01 43 72 24 01
///dragons.held.suitcase

5. Atelier C
123 Avenue Daumesnil, 12th;
www.atelierc.paris
///hits.stewing.outwit

Viaduc des Arts
///deed.rejected.scans

DRINK

Parisians live much of their lives in bars and cafés, where days are spent people-watching from pavement terraces and nights pass conversing with friends over a leisurely tipple.

Coffee Shops

*When you can lounge on a patio terrace or enjoy the
cosy hum of a café, why get your coffee to go? There's
nothing like sipping a fresh brew while watching
the world go by alongside the locals.*

YELLOW TUCAN

**Map 2; 20 Rue des Tournelles, 4th; ///zooms.factories.bronzed;
www.yellowtucan.com**

Around the corner from Place des Vosges is one of the Marais'
best-kept secrets for speciality coffee. Owner Vincent is always up
for a chat, so students pop in to natter under the pretence of catching
up on their reading. With big windows and tables decorated with
flowers, it's a calm place to draw breath on a busy day.

CHEZ PRUNE

Map 5; 36 Rue Beaurepaire, 10th; ///start.tools.translate; 01 42 41 30 47

This seemingly prosaic café is a canalside institution. Year after year,
everyone shuns the awning-shaded terrace of the latest opening to
wait in line for a scuffed metal chair on the pavement here. Stir at
least one sugar in your espresso (the only thing to order) and sip it in a
cloud of cigarette smoke for a quintessentially Parisian start to the day.

HANOÏ CORNER

Map 4; 7 Rue Blanche, 9th; ///gather.ponies.crew; www. hanoicorner.fr

Given the role France played in bringing coffee to Vietnam, it's surprising that contemporary Vietnamese coffee culture hasn't made greater inroads in Paris. Hoping to change that is this teeny café, where dark, intense coffee is served to an in-crowd.

» Don't leave without trying a cup of frothy, tiramisu-esque *café de Hanoi*, a traditional recipe made with eggs and condensed milk.

BACK IN BLACK

**Map 3; 25 Rue Amelot, 11th; ///charm.dilute.pits;
www. backinblackcoffee.com**

There's something almost scientific about the second café-roastery from renowned Parisian coffee pioneers KB. Staff are impeccably smart, measuring out beans and frothing milk with laboratory precision, while hipster patrons wait on restaurant-style seating. The single-origin coffee menu is one of the city's most extensive, and the grilled cheese sandwiches help to calm the stormiest of coffee shakes.

Try it!
BREW A CUP

If you can't get enough of Back in Black's divine brews, you can learn the art of roasting and cupping (coffee tasting) at one of its two-hour workshops. Check the website to find out the latest dates.

Solo, Pair, Crowd

A day in Paris without coffee is simply unthinkable. Get your fix to go or get comfy on a couch indoors.

FLYING SOLO
On the go
Grab a rich and aromatic espresso from Italian-run Pozzetto in the 4th and drink it as you wander the cobblestone streets of the Marais.

IN A PAIR
Bath time
If all that walking around town has you exhausted, put your feet up in a claw-foot tub (yep, it doubles as a seat here) and sip on good coffee at Le Pavillon des Canaux, a quirky café in the 19th with the vibe of an eclectic city-centre home.

FOR A CROWD
Coffee with a soundtrack
Stop by community coffee shop and Southeast Asian canteen The Hood in the 11th for a coffee with a banh mi. If you have a musical talent in your midst, there are instruments lying around to be played.

TREIZE AU JARDIN

Map 1; 5 Rue de Médicis, 6th; ///dynamic.jolly.instance;
www.treizeaujardin.com

A real homely feel pervades this Swedish-American-run bakery, from the warm welcome to its snug nooks. It's a meeting place for the expat community that have called this area home since the 1920s, but the Southern hospitality has drawn Paris-born crowds in their droves, too.
» Don't leave without trying one of the bakery's famous American classics: a pecan-chocolate cookie to tuck into between coffee sips.

CAFÉOTHÈQUE

Map 2; 52 Rue de l'Hôtel de Ville, 4th; ///tougher.water.moves;
www.lacafeotheque.com

There was once a time when ordering a cappuccino in Paris would be met with a raised eyebrow – and the quality of a good coffee was measured in bitterness and strength alone. We have Caféothèque to thank for paving the way for change. You'll be hard-pressed to find a Parisian who hasn't whiled away an afternoon cradling a rich brew at Gloria Monténégro's cosy temple to new-wave coffee.

CAFÉ PIMPIN

Map 4; 64 Rue Ramey, 18th; ///slice.steeped.closets; 01 46 06 97 25

The area around the Sacré-Cœur may no longer be the village it was in Van Gogh's day, but nearby Jules Joffrin, where this café abides, is the modern equivalent. Instead of sipping absinthe in bordels and bars, these days folks catch up over chai lattes in cute spots like this.

Wine Bars

Meeting friends for a glass of wine is the post-work catch-up event of choice. Something to snack on as you drink is customary, whether it's a few almonds or a cheese board to work through into the night.

LA BELLE HORTENSE

Map 2; 31 Rue Vieille du Temple, 3rd; ///fencing.disclose.swinging; www.cafeine.com/fr/belle-hortense

Merging good books with good wine, this timeless spot is so special that literature lovers can't resist showing it off to friends visiting from abroad. From the moment you set eyes on the vintage indigo-blue

Shh!

Nestled in the corner of the oldest covered walkway in the city is Coinstot Vino *(22–30 Galerie Montmartre)*, a laid-back bar that is hidden well enough to be missed. Shelves packed with divine elixir reflect an extensive cellar selection, including a substantial organic range. Opt for the "wine by glass" list and savour each sip on the unique interior terrace. Who needs a sommelier for a full winery experience?

façade, its window full of colourful books and a variety of spirits, you're staying put for the night. Inside, regulars engage in debates at the bar while intellectuals sip on fine wine and browse the wooden bookshelves. Blend in with a glass of the "wine of the month", settle on a stool in the cosy space and live the Parisian bohemian dream.

POMPETTE

Map 4; 15 Rue Hippolyte Lebas, 9th; ///readings.polite.dices;
www.pompetteparis.com

Many Parisians claim never to have one too many, but at Pompette you're practically encouraged to (elegantly) over-indulge and get a bit tipsy – "pompette" means just that in French. Run by an Australian, French and Canadian team, the 28-seat bar (yes, you'll need to book ahead) has a seriously exciting natural wine list (that's wine made with minimal intervention on a small scale) and a tasty food menu to match.
» Don't leave without trying a bottle of Pet Nat – fizz made by the ancestral method – from winemaker Christian Binner.

DEV!ANT

Map 4; 39 Rue des Petites Écuries, 10th;
///packages.grownup.exam; www.deviant.paris

No seats? No problem. There's not a single stool or chair at this mirror-walled bar, open entirely onto the street. Instead, trendy Parisians gather at the slim marble counters, drinking their way through bottles of Rue de la Soif Sauvignon Blanc or unusual Austrian rosés poured by a young team with attitude (and enviable wine knowledge).

MR ALPHONSE

Map 3; 8 Rue de la Folie Méricourt, 11th;
///because.striving.empire; 06 08 73 63 72

When almost every table is booked out on a Friday night, you know you're onto a good thing. With a living-room-style cellar perfect for groups, Mr Alphonse is the father-and-son-run wine bar you wish was at the end of your road. The enormous charcuterie platters are made to share, and there's no unnecessarily encyclopaedic wine list.

FREDDY'S

Map 1; 54 Rue de Seine, 6th; ///mailing.piglet.those

There's not a hint of snobbery at this Brooklyn-esque bar with its stone walls, wooden stalls and lively crowd. Those inclined to panic in the presence of haughty sommeliers will find the welcoming, English-speaking staff handy given the extensive choice of wines by the glass.

LE BARON ROUGE

Map 3; 1 Rue Théophile Roussel, 12th; ///marker.risen.possibly;
www.lebaronrouge.net

The cheapest thimble-sized glasses of wine in Paris are drunk standing up at barrel tables at this Aligre institution. During the day you'll join traders from the adjacent marché *(p84)*, at night mates enjoying an easy-going *apéro*. There's a wide range of wines listed on chalkboards, but take too long to decide and you'll lose your place in the queue.

» Don't leave without trying a platter of oysters, shucked just outside the bar at the weekend when in season, paired with a glass of Chablis.

Liked by the locals

"Mr Alphonse is my go-to spot
for an after-work drink or *apéro*.
The wine list is interesting
and diverse, the atmosphere
relaxed and the cheeses delicious
(try my favourite, the burrata
with truffle oil)."

JOCELYN CLARK, WINE GUIDE

Cocktail Joints

*While wine is made to be enjoyed with a meal in
Paris, cocktails are an art deserving sole attention.
Serious mixology is often a special occasion splurge,
with only the best bars dedicated to the craft.*

BISOU

Map 2; 15 Boulevard du Temple, 3rd;
///gaps.mime.chickens; www.bar-bisou.fr

There's no menu at this self-styled sexy spot, so get chatting to
the staff for a drink tailored to your mood and preferences. If €10
creations weren't good enough, all non-alcoholic ingredients are
seasonal and sourced in France, and leftover fruits get transformed
into garnishes as part of a zero-waste policy.

CAFÉ CHÉRI(E)

Map 5; 44 Boulevard de la Villette, 19th;
///hobbit.upstairs.actor; 09 53 05 93 36

Topping the list of Belleville's social spots is this instantly recognizable
red bar, where hip young locals welcome the easy-going vibe and
bargain cocktails. Take a seat at one of the classroom-style tables
and observe the shifting ambience as if you're at a house party.

DIRTY LEMON

Map 3; 24 Rue de la Folie Méricourt, 11th; ///napkins.asks.sound; www.dirtylemonbar.com

This spot has redefined the cocktail bar, creating a new kind of female-run and inclusive space that was lacking on the Paris scene. Turning over-fussy menus on their head with cheekily named drinks like Soft Butch and Trophy Wife has made Dirty Lemon a firm stomping ground for groups of girlfriends and an LGBTQ+ clientele. **» Don't leave without** trying the Cougar, an intriguing mix of yellow pepper juice, paprika and chorizo-infused tequila.

LITTLE RED DOOR

Map 2; 60 Rue Charlot, 3rd; ///pining.elder.rainbow; www.lrdparis.com

Since it opened in 2012, this speakeasy-style spot has been listed mutliple times on the World's 50 Best Bars. Why? It probably has something to do with the low-lit, cosy ambience and the "farm-to-glass" cocktail list, influenced heavily by French produce. The menu changes each year, too, so there's always something new to try.

Try it!
SHAKE IT UP

If you've learned a thing or two watching mixologists, head to speciality spirits shop Esprit 50cl *(www.esprit50cl.fr)* in the 11th to pick up unusual French-made spirits to make your own cocktails at home.

Liked by the locals

"While many Parisians choose to gather at the riverbank to enjoy drinks on sunny days, there really is nothing like sipping a cocktail on the *terrasse* of a Parisian café and gazing at the lively streets."

AGNES BAREILLE, PUBLIC TRANSPORTATION
PROJECT MANAGER

LA COMMUNE

Map 5; 80 Boulevard de Belleville, 20th;
///guessing.modules.petal; https://la-commune.zenchef.com

Winning cocktail combinations don't get much better than chalice-like punch bowls served to share in a lovely fairy-light-lit, plant-filled conservatory. A tropical vibe pervades here year-round, fuelled by generous ladles of rum punch and a banging hip-hop soundtrack.

LULU WHITE

Map 4; 12 Rue Frochot, 9th; ///minority.bake.herring; www.luluwhite.bar

Almost every kind of late-night revelry can be found on rowdy Rue Frochot, yet it's still somewhat of a surprise to find a New Orleans-inspired speakeasy among the road's drinking dens. This classy spot has prices to match, but a night of Ramos-gin-fizz-fuelled fun awaits. The decor – velvet booths and mirrored ceilings – is a little bit over the top and a little bit luxe, much like the clientele.

» **Don't leave without** trying an absinthe flight. It's not hallucinogenic like it was during the belle époque, but it still packs a punch.

LAVOMATIC

Map 2; 30 Rue René Boulanger, 10th; ///blubber.nearly.sank;
www.lavomatic.paris

This isn't your usual speakeasy. Sure, it has a hidden entrance (behind a washing machine in an old laundromat). But there's no moody vibe here. Instead, you'll be greeted by a bright space filled with Brillo pad-themed stools and colourful cocktails – there's even a swing seat.

Breweries and Wineries

France has always celebrated its regional wines and beers, but few had been made in Paris until the last decade or so. With this change came a raft of innovative businesses (and excited punters to match).

BRASSERIE DE LA GOUTTE D'OR

Map 4; 28 Rue de la Goutte d'Or, 18th; ///collect.unable.oblige; www.brasserielagouttedor.com

The beers brewed here may be staples on grocery store shelves across Paris, but nothing beats visiting the brand's taproom, usually open three days a week. Staunch fans come to get the inside scoop from the team – oh, and to brag about being one of the first to taste the latest, locally sourced creations.

LES CUVES DE FAUVE

Map 3; 64 Rue de Charonne, 11th; ///puns.pinches.deny; www.fauvebiere.com

Colourful, fun and free from beer-bro culture, this bright brewpub shows how far the scene has come. On sunny days, drinkers spill out onto the terrace beneath the blue awnings, soaking up the rays and sipping one of the rotating sixteen beers on tap – all brewed on site. If you somehow haven't got your beer fix yet, the burgers and fries come with toppings like reblochon and shallots confited in IPA.

» **Don't leave without** trying the Fleur Noire, a chocolatey imperial stout flavoured with vanilla beans, cocoa nibs and tonka beans.

LA VIGNE DE SURESNES
Map 6; 4 Rue du Passage Saint-Maurice, Suresnes;
///booster.fight.liver; 01 47 98 90 18

Just beyond the city limits proper, across the Seine from the Bois de Boulogne, is this bijou winery. But with the Eiffel Tower as the backdrop to the vines, Paris doesn't feel too far away. Scooping awards for its Chardonnay-Sauvignon blends, La Vigne de Suresnes honours the long tradition of great wine made in Suresnes – beloved by monarchs in the 1500s and 1600s. Book a tour and tasting to find out why.

Shh!

La Winerie Parisienne is the big gun of the Parisian winemaking scene, its bottles appearing on bar menus all over the city. That's not the only way to taste the blends, though. The brand's winery out in Montreuil isn't routinely open to visitors, but its umbrella group, Paris Maison de Vins, also encompasses the Domaine la Bouche du Roi – just outside the city on the Plaine de Versailles, and open for visits. Find out about its latest adventures and tastings at www.winerieparisienne.fr.

PANAME BREWING COMPANY

Map 5; 41 bis Quai de la Loire, 19th; ///implore.lateral.vote;
www.panamebrewingcompany.com

Perhaps the best-known of all the micro-breweries in Paris (thanks to its enormous floating terrace at the top of the Bassin de la Villette), Paname lives up to its hype. With great views over the water and an airy, industrial indoor space, it's popular day and night with large groups of all ages who come to watch the sightseeing boats ply up and down the canal while tasting their way through the pale ales.

» Don't leave without trying the Brexiteer: a delicious IPA (and friendly dig at the Brits) to mark the UK's departure from the EU.

LA FINE MOUSSE

Map 3; 4 bis Avenue Jean Aicard, 11th; ///dragons.inspector.part;
www.lafinemousse.fr

Split into a bar and restaurant facing each other, this spot has all the requisites for serious beer geeks to practically move in. One of the city's original champions of craft beer, La Fine Mousse has built a

Try it!
TAKE A BREWERY TOUR

Oberkampf's BAPBAP brewery *(www.bap bap.paris)* in the 11th is one of the few to offer tours in English. They run on Fridays and offer an introduction to the brewing process – as well as a tasting, of course.

city-wide reputation by pouring niche beers from France, Belgium, Sweden and beyond in this pleasing backstreet pocket of the 11th. On the north side is the bar, where a relaxed vibe slowly turns lively as punters test 20 different options on tap (plus many more by the bottle). On the south side is the restaurant, where things get more serious, with a six-course tasting menu waiting to soak up that beer.

VIGNERONS PARISIENS

Map 2; 55 Rue de Turbigo, 3rd; ///business.slides.only; www.lesvignerons.paris

Some 60 years after the last large-scale cellars closed at Bercy, the owners behind this urban micro-winery are bringing winemaking back to the heart of Paris with a whole lot of love. During a tasting session, you'll find out how Matthieu, Emmanuel and Frédéric bring their grapes to Paris and ferment their boutique range of reds and whites in this bijou space. It's one to show off to visiting parents.

BAR GALLIA

Map 6; 35 Rue Méhul, Pantin; ///grain.student.vent; www.galliaparis.com

Even some life-long Parisians have yet to tread outside the city limits to up-and-coming semi-suburb Pantin. They really should hurry up and get a move on, though, even if it's just to visit Bar Gallia (of the brewery of the same name). Those in the know jump on the metro to join everyone from millennials to an older "bobo" (bourgeois-bohemian) crowd, who congregate in the beer garden on a mission to drink the place dry.

Unmissable Terraces

The terrasse *is a Paris institution – so much so that alfresco spots are tough to score on sunny days. Imagine cafés under umbrellas lining cobblestone streets and year-round people-watching. Divine.*

LE PROGRÈS

Map 2; 1 Rue de Bretagne, 3rd; ///dance.teaspoons.special; 01 42 72 01 44
Chattering students and fashion interns fill the tables under the signature red awnings of this corner café. The theme is young and trendy for the most part, but keep an eye open: this place feels plucked out of the 1960s, and some patrons seem like extras in a film. It's a neighbourhood go-to with no-frills coffee and cold beer, and bustling Rue de Bretagne offering up all the entertainment you need.

LA SARDINE

Map 5; 32 Rue Sainte-Marthe, 10th; ///snatched.reveal.badly
Belleville's "bobo" (bourgeois-bohemian) locals are a little bit in love with this cute tapas-and-wine bar, which sits on the quaint, tree-shaded Place Sainte-Marthe. Grab one of the brightly coloured chairs that cascade onto the square, order a drink and sit back to watch the world go by. You'll have lots of company: as the sun goes

La Sardine hosts live music occasionally throughout the year – see their socials for more information.

down, groups of friends gather in droves here, snacking on plates of tapas and sipping on aromatic organic wines. Expect a buzzing vibe till late.

GRANDE MOSQUÉE DE PARIS

Map 6; 39 Rue Geoffroy-Saint-Hillaire, 5th;

///dine.fizzled.actual; www.la-mosquee.com/le-salon-de-the

So it's not quite on the pavement, but rather in a secluded, leafy courtyard that makes it feel like a true find for those who stumble upon it. Serving up €2 mint tea and North African pastries, the mosque's charming café truly transports you to Morocco. Birds flutter around the tiled tables picking up crumbs, while locals wave for more of the sweet tea and bask in a moment of tranquillity.

» Don't leave without trying the traditional North African pastries flavoured with pistachio and orange-blossom.

COMPTOIR DES ARCHIVES

Map 2; 41 Rue des Archives, 3rd; ///begin.sloping.perform;

https://le-comptoir-des-archives.business.site/

It's hard to miss this corner café when strolling down one of the two major thoroughfares it covers. In the morning, you'll see regulars stopping by for a quick espresso before the working day starts; return in the afternoon and it's the haunt of passersby, who sip on mint lemonades. Pop by for a simple drink and stay to take in the foot traffic on the adjoining Rue des Archives and Rue Rambuteau.

LES PHILOSOPHES CAFÉ

Map 2; 28 Rue Vieille du Temple, 4th; ///release.memory.memory;
www.cafeine.com/en/philosophes

There's something charming about the terrace of this classic French
bistro in the winter, when retirees cosy up in their scarves, lingering
over a glass of affordable house wine and watching the comings
and goings of the colourful Marais district. A selection of proudly
homemade small dishes make this an all-day-and-night place to
nibble, sip and watch.

LA MARINE

Map 5; 55 bis Quai de Valmy, 10th; ///above.infects.costs;
www.lamarinecanalsaintmartin.com

This archetypical corner café, overlooking the Canal Saint-Martin, is
the kind of place that you pop into for a low-key lunchtime salad, only
for an hour to turn into three, and the salad plate to be replaced with

Shh!

Coffee shop KB in the 9th (62
Rue des Martyrs) is well known
to Mac-wielding locals, but as
they set up stations inside, the
lucky few know the best spot is
on the terrace outside. Set back
from the traffic, it's perfect for
watching all manner of crowds
coming up the hilly street.
Secure a seat, head in to order,
then sip your coffee – it's the
good stuff – once it arrives, with
a somewhat smug feeling while
freelancers work indoors.

a cognac. The waterfront tables here are in high demand year round, thanks to the perfect side-by-side seating, letting you continue to chat while watching others stroll alongside the water. The drink menu plays all the greatest hits, tempting you to linger beyond that cognac.

LA PLACE VERTE

Map 3; 105 Rue Oberkampf, 11th; ///palaces.chop.flags; 01 43 57 34 10

Large terraces are so rare in this district that those in the know rush to claim a table here on sunny days before everyone else cottons on. An official street art project takes up space on the corner – courtesy of cutting-edge creatives – providing an urban backdrop to the constant chatter and spirited laughter in the air The wall art is renewed bi-monthly, should you need an excuse to return.

LA ROTONDE STALINGRAD

Map 5; 6–8 Place de la Bataille de Stalingrad, 19th; ///mondays.liberty.crowned; www.arotondestalingrad.com

Far from the tourist draws, this remnant of the old city wall is home to an expansive terrace. As soon as summer hits, young professionals pack into lounge chairs under umbrellas to sip a mojito and mingle. It's the people you meet who shape a visit at this atmospheric terrace, where it always feels like Saturday night no matter the time of day.

» Don't leave without trying a kebab from the Mediterranean food kiosk that sets up a stand on the adjacent square. They're gourmet, and a step up from the usual street-side vendors in Paris.

**Settle in at
MARLUSSE ET LAPIN**

Snag one of the swing seats at this dive bar where bohemians hang out in Montmartre today (absinthe sometimes included).

18TH

BLVD DE LA CHAPELLE

3

BLVD DE CLICHY

*In the early 20th century, many people visited the **Moulin Rouge** for easily obtainable absinthe and opium as much as for the shows.*

PIGALLE

RUE CONDORCET

BOULEVARD

RUE DU FAUBOURG ST-DENIS

RUE BLANCHE

9TH

DE

MAGENTA

10TH

8TH

SQUARE DE LA TRINITÉ

LA   FAYETTE

RUE

RUE D'HAUTEVILLE

**Step back in time at
HARRY'S NEW
YORK BAR**

Get cosy in this wood-panelled bar, where the French 75 and the Bloody Mary were invented. Order one for you and the other for your pal.

BLVD HAUSSMANN

**Get in the spirit at
LE SYNDICAT**

4

PL DE L'OPÉRA

2

2ND

Get a taste of contemporary cocktail culture at this innovative bar, where old-fashioned French spirits are revived in unique concoctions.

BLVD ST-MARTIN

1

RUE DE TURBIGO

**Learn the secrets at
THE RITZ**

Splash out on a masterclass in cocktail-making – and delve into the lives of the Ritz's illustrious guests – with Colin Peter Field.

Bar Hemingway
is named in the writer's honour – a place where he drank 51 martinis in a row to celebrate Paris's liberation after WWII.

3RD

BLVD DE SÉBASTOPOL

MARAIS

7TH

BOULEVARD

ST-GERMAIN

BOULEVARD

RASPAIL

INVALIDES

La Seine

6TH

4TH

RUE

DE

RIVOLI

Île de la Cité

Île St-Louis

LATIN
QUARTER

5TH

0 metres   500
0 yards   500

An evening of
cocktail culture

Wine may be the tipple most associated with Paris, but many great cocktails (sidecar, momosa, rose) were born here. Paris is, after all, where some of the world's most talented artists spent nights fuelled by absinthe, and where the "Lost Generation" partied so hard that Parisians have spent another two generations trying to recreate their excesses. The city is by no means trapped in the 1920s, but you can't sip cocktails in the 2020s without travelling through a century of mixology – just pace yourself.

1. The Ritz
15 Place Vendôme, 1st;
www.ritzescoffier.com
///video.fuzzy.ticked

2. Harry's New York Bar
5 Rue Daunou, 2nd;
www.harrysbar.fr
///bliss.qualified.approve

3. Marlusse et Lapin
14 Rue Germain Pilon, 18th;
01 42 59 17 97
///brighter.success.bunkers

4. Le Syndicat
51 Rue du Faubourg Saint-Denis, 10th; www.syndicat
cocktailclub.com
///sifts.retrain.bright

5. Moonshiner
5 Rue Sedaine, 11th;
www.moonshinerbar.fr
///apron.sang.youthful

Bar Hemingway
///compiled.edges.opens

Moulin Rouge
///enforced.takes.sling

On the map (labels)

BLVD DE LA VILLETTE

BLVD RICHARD LENOIR

LACE
E LA
JBLIQUE

BLVD DU
MPLE

11TH

**Nightcap at
MOONSHINER**
Push open the fridge inside Pizza Da Vito and enter Paris's first speakeasy: a dimly lit, jazz-playing bar.

5

BLVD BEAUMARCHAIS

PL. DE LA
BASTILLE

BASTILLE

SHOP

Scouting the best produce at an open-air market, designing your own scent, hunting for one-of-a-kind outfits – shopping is one of life's simple pleasures in Paris.

Gourmet Treats

Foodie fans with a finesse for fine dining, Parisians are never short of quality produce in their cuisine. Specialist gourmet shops are the place to go in search of delicious ingredients and edible gifts.

CONFITURE PARISIENNE

Map 3; 17 Avenue Daumesnil, 12th; ///angle.dished.locating; www.confiture-parisienne.com

Though Parisians rarely eat breakfast (many just survive on a strong shot of coffee), when they do, they do it in style. Join the preserve connoisseurs and peruse the quirky flavours of jam (carrot and vanilla anyone?) in this high-end shop under the arches of the Coulée Verte. Invest in a pretty pot and you're sure to make any home brunch boujee.

Try it!
JAM FROM SCRATCH

Got a serious sweet tooth? Book a spot at one of Confiture Parisienne's monthly jam-making classes. You'll find out some of their secrets and leave with your own personalized jar to take home.

MAISON PLISSON

Map 2; 93 Boulevard Beaumarchais, 3rd; ///grin.spent.dented;
www.lamaisonplisson.com

This beloved luxury food hall offers a gourmet shopping experience like no other. Upstairs you'll find locally produced veg, meat and cheese, while downstairs is a gold mine of jars, tins and bottles to take home. It's pricey, but foodies will tell you it's worth it.

» **Don't leave without** buying a few of their smart "tartinables" to spread on toast for *apéro*: the truffled artichoke cream is a knock-out.

TAKA & VERMO

Map 5; 61 bis Rue du Faubourg Saint-Denis, 10th;
///dine.fakes.stuffing; www.takavermo.fr

While doing their weekly shop, locals often pop by this artisan cheese store for a treat. The cheese here is sustainably sourced and hand-selected (or made in-house) by its young owners, Laure Takahashi and Mathieu Vermorel – self-confessed fromage fanatics. It's a lovely place to grab some treats for a picnic in nearby Jardin Villemin.

LE VIN AU VERT

Map 4; 70 Rue de Dunkerque, 9th; ///steadily.rocky.flow; 01 83 56 46 93

A wine shop by day and restaurant at dinner, Le Vin au Vert is a popular destination among wine sellers and makers, renowned for its natural wines and generous Jura allocations. Set between the insalubrious streets around Barbès and the pretty Square d'Anvers, it's the kind of place you'll only stumble upon if you come searching.

E. DEHILLERIN

Map 1; 18–20 Rue Coquillière, 1st; ///slippers.alarmed.glow;
www.edehillerin.fr

If Ratatouille were to go kitchenware shopping in Paris, he'd head to
E. Dehillerin. This is the city's temple to cookware, and reverence is
wholly encouraged. With few visible prices and little signage, it's near
impossible to navigate and can be ruinously expensive – but standing
perplexed beneath the towering racks of plush pans is all part of the
experience. Top tip: the sturdy copper pans will last a lifetime.

BMK

Map 5; 14 Rue de la Fidélité, 10th; ///funded.silly.panthers;
www.bmkparis.com

Come lunch or dinner, cool young couples and vegan friends head to
this hipster hangout for some of Paris's best African cuisine. There's a
small *épicerie* (grocery) hidden here, too, where you can pick up some
of the ingredients that make BMK's homemade dishes so delicious.
The products change seasonally and are based on availability,
ranging from tamarind jam to organic Ethiopian coffee. Pop by to
pick up a gift and you'll probably find yourself staying for some food.

VELAN

Map 5; 87 Passage Brady, 10th; ///buck.gangs.passages; www.velan.paris

This beloved grocery store has been a fixture inside Passage Brady
(p178), a centre for local Indian and Pakistani communities, for forty
years and has a wide fanbase to show for it. Initiated regulars come to

this treasure trove to stock up on different kinds of pepper, cassava, chutneys and a host of spices to amplify the flavours in their dishes. There's no better stop for Indian specialties.

A LA VILLE DE RODEZ

Map 2; 22 Rue Vieille du Temple, 4th; ///bridges.uptown.spreads; 01 48 87 79 36

As the rest of the Marais has gentrified, it's a testament to the quality of A la Ville de Rodez's products that this deli has changed little over the past hundred years – *saucissons* still dangle from the ceiling and window displays are laden with pâté. It's been family-run for generations (they live upstairs) and their passion for regional produce is shared by their loyal clientele, many of whom will give you tips on what to buy.

» Don't leave without buying a slice of St Nectaire, an earthy, washed-rind cheese that's one of the best specialities of the Auvergne.

Shh!

Stop by Edwart Chocolatier (*www.edwart.fr*) in the Marais and ask to try some sugary samples. It doesn't advertise this, but you're welcome to taste the jewel-like creations (the curry praline chocolate is a great choice). Chocolate maker Edwin Yansané, often working the counter, is as friendly as his products are magical. Consider buying a box of ganaches or one of the fantastic chocolate spreads, including a salted caramel sauce that likely won't survive the journey home.

Beloved Markets

*Outdoor and covered markets are the cornerstone
of local life, with one gracing every arrondissement.
Whether it's for bric-a-brac, vintage items or fresh
produce, remember to bring a canvas bag (or five).*

MARCHÉ D'ALIGRE

**Map 3; Place d'Aligre, 12th; ///reclaim.dabbled.alarmed;
www.marchedaligre.free.fr**

You can't beat this one. You just can't. This stretch of outdoor food stalls,
a covered indoor hall and an adjacent flea market opens six days a
week. On Saturday and Sunday mornings, join the crush of Parisians
with their caddies and canvas bags as they do their weekly produce
shopping. Sellers shout the day's deals as customers grab and bag
their own fruit and vegetables. If ever there were a place to get
pushed away by an older Parisian woman, this is it.

MARCHÉ PRÉSIDENT-WILSON

Map 6; Avenue du Président Wilson, 16th; ///silently.magical.many

By virtue of its location in a ritzy district, this twice-weekly open-air
market is where you'll find the most gourmet of Parisians. Renowned
Michelin star chefs order their seasonal vegetables here and chichi

Make for Rungis, Europe's largest wholesale market, where chefs also source their food.

locals come to pick up refined supplies for dinner parties. It's not pretentious, though: here, joyful vendors tempt customers with tasting platters and a side of banter.

MARCHÉ SAINT-PIERRE

Map 4; 2 Rue Charles Nodier, 18th; ///empty.spiking.fired;
www.marchesaintpierre.com

Fancy making some cool new cushion covers? Always wanted to design your own fashion line? In the shadow of the Sacré-Cœur, this warren-like complex, spread out over six floors, seems to feature every fabric in the world to get you started. The couturiers and student seamstresses who venture inside always leave with a few metres for a home décor or fashion project.

MARCHÉ SAINT-MARTIN

Map 5; 31/33 Rue du Château d'Eau, 10th; ///tender.villas.joins;
www.marchesaintmartin.com

This humble covered market doesn't usually make it into the guides, but to overlook it would be a shame. Here, English exists in rare whispers among accidental tourists, who wander in from the nearby Eurostar terminal at Gare du Nord. Moving swiftly past them are easy-going locals, who dip into German grocery boutiques and pick up fresh flowers during their work breaks.

» Don't leave without buying a portion of tangy goat cheese from Laurent Bouvet, the artisan cheese vendor.

MARCHÉ AUX PUCES DE LA PORTE DE VANVES

Map 6; Avenue Georges Lafenestre, 14th; ///surviving.unto.bubbles; www.pucesdevanves.fr

Every weekend, bargain hunters descend on the city's most lively flea market, spread over two avenues. Breezy traders set up shop on wonky tables, awaiting the French celebs and niche collectors who bargain with them over an endless variety of odds and ends. Arrive early, bring cash and remember a few sturdy tote bags – you'll need them to carry home the old-school folk art and antique perfume bottles you'll find.

VILLAGE SAINT-PAUL

Map 2; 20 Rue Saint-Paul, 4th; ///charted.able.decoder

This calm tangle of courtyards, tucked between the Marais and the Seine, houses antique stores, a hat maker and even a shop dedicated to locally sourced inventions. Village Saint-Paul mercifully lacks the

Shh!

At the corner of Gabriel and Marigny avenues lies a heaven for philatelists (aka people who collect postage stamps). Set up in the late 19th century, when stamp collecting was a popular hobby for trendy young Parisiens, this spot is the haunt of both serious collectors and bemused tourists who have stumbled in from the nearby Champs-Elysées. Join them browsing the stalls, open Thursdays and at weekends.

stress of the more popular shopping venues, providing an oasis for browsing without pressure. There's a friendly, community vibe to it, where chatting with a shopkeeper as you admire artisan wallpaper and a bit of haggling with the dealers is all to be expected. Plus, there are a few laidback cafés to settle into when the shopping is done.

» **Don't leave without** checking the schedule to time your visit with a *brocante* or *vide grenier*, flea markets that pop up here once a month.

MARCHÉ DEJEAN

Map 4; Rue Dejean, 18th; ///purses.neutron.pints

Aromas of strong spices and the sounds of vendors bartering envelop you as soon as you hit the area known as "Little Africa". A North and West African community has lived in the Goutte d'Or neighbourhood for decades (hence the nickname), and this busy market exists as a hub for these residents. Families and friends come here to browse the generously brimming stalls, stocking up on ingredients like bissap, tiof, manioc, igname and gombo (to name just a few) that are essential for making traditional African dishes.

MARCHÉ BIOLOGIQUE DES BATIGNOLLES

Map 4; 34 Boulevard des Batignolles, 8th; ///protect.discount.quibble

Buying bio – aka organic – borders on an obsession in Paris. Save yourself the trouble of hopping from greengrocer to deli and stop by this Saturday food market instead. It's a regular haunt of well-to-do couples, who pop in to pick up Spanish ham or artisanal honey.

Home Touches

Parisians may have notoriously tiny apartments, but their desire for style means they still devour a good concept or homeware store. Pop by one to pick up your own chic piece of Paris to bring home.

SERGEANT PAPER

Map 5; 26 Rue du Château d'Eau, 10th; ///tangible.clots.mincing; www.sergeantpaper.com

Follow in the footsteps of the city's young aesthetes and upgrade your home with some funky limited-edition prints from Sergeant Paper. This pop art boutique and gallery is a hotspot for art graduates and upcoming illustrators (you may even spot some proud patrons gazing up at their own art on display). Bag one of over 900 original and

Try it!
CREATE A CANDLE

You can channel self-care while caring for the environment on a vegan candle-making course with maker Justine de Ponoie. Search for her course details on www.wecandoo.fr.

affordable – prices start at just two figures – artworks to pop on your wall and you may just pass as Parisian. Your purchased print comes with a certificate of authenticity so you can brag to your pals.

LA TRÉSORERIE

Map 5; 11 Rue du Château d'Eau, 10th; ///debate.belong.meanest; www.latresorerie.fr

Design-forward Parisians happy to splash a bit of cash on functional, albeit very pretty, homeware come here for the crockery, glassware and textiles. A third of products are made in France and the rest in Europe, so there's a hint of sustainability in all of it too. Chances are you'll find something useful for around the house – perhaps in a new aesthetic you never knew you really embodied (Paris can do that).

» Don't leave without checking out the cosmetics section, which stocks a mixure of zero-waste items and locally made products.

FLEUX

Map 2; 52 Rue Sainte-Croix de la Bretonnerie, 4th; ///monopoly.occurs.edits; www.fleux.com

No local studio is complete without a set of espresso cups or plant pots from this Marais-born homeware emporium. Fleux's aesthetic is hard to pinpoint and it's anything but understated. You'll find everything here: handmade ceramics, table linens, beeswax wraps, novelty socks and quirky printed totes (perfect for showing off when you pick up your groceries). If you're looking for muted colours and classic French design, head elsewhere: Fleux is big on personality.

MERCI

Map 2; 111 Boulevard Beaumarchais, 3rd; ///skewed.warriors.drum;
www.merci-merci.com

Ask any Parisian who the *crème de la crème* of homeware design is
and they're bound to name Merci. The *grand magasin* of concept
stores may have spawned a number of offshoot concepts, but it's
always important to honour the original. It's also got a healthy conscience, actively funding educational projects in Madagascar.

» Don't leave without taking a break in the café filled with countless
second-hand books that you can leaf through (it's one of three on site).

CSAO

Map 2; 9 Rue Elzevir, 3rd; ///coverage.driving.lofts; www.csao.fr

Truly homemade products are hard to come by in Paris, but head
to CSAO and you'll be spoilt for choice. This shop stocks colourful,
ethically created homeware and décor, all individually crafted by
West African artisans. Yes they carry a certain price tag, but you'll
feel good knowing proceeds go back to social projects in Senegal.

AILLEURS

Map 3; 17 Rue Saint Nicolas, 12th; ///hometown.together.managed;
www.ailleurs-paris.com

Looking to achieve that rustic French look in your kitchen? Tablescapes
and stylized glassware are just a few of the items that line this concept
shop. The owner is a graduate of Merci, so the pedigree is reliable – as
the design elite who pensively browse the tasteful items will vouch for.

Liked by the locals

"People should visit our boutique because it's a trip to West Africa in the heart of the Marais – a trip in colours and patterns, full of gaiety."

ONDINE SAGLIO, CO-OWNER OF CSAO

Books and Stationery

Every creative dreams of living out a humble existence in Paris. Scribbling away in a notebook on a pavement terrace or dipping into a French novel underneath stacked shelves is as bohemian as it gets.

LIBRAIRIE GALIGNANI

Map 1; 224 Rue de Rivoli, 1st; ///fleet.ribs.brains; www.galignani.fr

Since opening in 1801, this store – which claims to be the continent's oldest English bookshop – has developed a reputation as Paris's most "serious" nook. Despite its prestigious accolades, it's a friendly spot to get lost in. Expect to see booksellers climbing ladders to reach the highest shelf for customers, bibliophiles pondering a purchase in a leather armchair and the odd author hosting a talk.

PAPIER PLUS

Map 2; 9 Rue Pont Louis Philippe, 4th; ///soup.slipped.dogs; www.papierplus.com

The art of letter writing and journaling is alive and well in France, and this pretty store gives Parisians all the more reason to continue that tradition. Since 1976, Papier Plus has been designing stationery for serious writers, as well as those who want you to think they're serious. The minimalist items seem deceptively simple, but these are the little black dresses of paper products; investment pieces that will never fail you. The formats of the timeless monochromatic notebooks haven't changed, but the colours evolve over time, meaning there's something different to tempt you at every visit.

» **Don't leave without** buying the signature *carnet*. Moleskins are available everywhere, but these locally created notebooks aren't.

LIBRAIRIE JOUSSEAUME

Map 1; 45 Galerie Vivienne, 2nd; ///starred.spot.bucket;
www.librairie-jousseaume.fr

Galerie Vivienne *(p176)*, restored to its 19th-century glory, seems all the more historical with this old-world bookshop at its heart. Forgotten by locals who only remember it's there when wandering the covered passage, the rickety store survives despite a lack of notoriety. Browse rare history and poetry titles while scaling the winding staircase or opt for cheaper titles on racks in the gallery.

PRÉSENCE AFRICAINE

Map 2; 25 bis Rue des Écoles, 5th; ///form.sugar.promises;
www.presenceafricaine.com

The Latin Quarter seems to have a bookstore for every proclivity, and this visionary shop is one not to overlook. Part of a publishing house founded in 1949 to represent African authors, the store stocks fiction and non-fiction that amplify Black voices from Francophone Africa, so maybe skip Victor Hugo for a moment and try something new.

LES MOTS À LA BOUCHE

Map 3; 37 Rue Saint-Ambroise, 11th; ///patting.spin.weds;
www.motsbouche.com

Though gentrification ousted the city's only LGBTQ+ bookshop from its home in the Marais in 2020, it wasn't long before it reopened just outside the district. Whatever you're after – art, fiction, biography – you'll find it here, and if you can't, just ask the approachable staff. They love to chat about the unique stock and their favourite books.

PAPIER TIGRE

Map 2; 5 Rue des Filles du Calvaire, 3rd;
///gravest.openings.lemmings; www.papiertigre.fr

Parisians have long had a love affair with all things Japanese (think Monet and his water lilies), and this stationery shop is just the latest love note – pun intended. Everything is design-forward, from the notebooks with bold geometric patterns to the colourful pencils.

Shh!

Iconic Anglophone bookstore Shakespeare and Company *(www. shakespeareandcompany. com)* may be somewhat of a victim of its own success, but Parisians don't avoid this Left Bank stalwart on that account. Rather, they bypass the crowds during the day and mingle with local book lovers at niche Sunday events that many tourists don't know about, like feminist book clubs, embroidery sessions and jazz on the terrace outside.

LADY LONG SOLO

Map 3; 38 Rue Keller, 11th; ///wonderfully.nods.jumbled; www.ladylongsolo.com

This feminist bookshop isn't afraid to tackle big issues. Expect books discussing everything from class dynamics to colonialism. Regular talks by authors are hosted, too, touching on subjects like Black feminism and deconstructing romantic spaces.

L'EAU ET LES RÊVES

Map 5; 9 Quai de l'Oise, 19th; ///loosed.lunch.tender; www.penichelibrairie.com

Parisians will tell you that two of their most beloved pastimes are reading and lounging by the water. L'Eau et les Rêves was onto a good thing, then, when it opened over a decade ago as a floating bookshop on the Canal de l'Ourcq. The barge stocks lots of nature and travel titles, and hosts readings with upcoming French authors.

» Don't leave without having a coffee and a cake break aboard the boat. Your patronage helps keep this venue afloat (ahem).

THE RED WHEELBARROW

Map 1; 9 Rue de Médicis, 6th; ///puffed.riper.limit; www.theredwheelbarrowbookstore.com

This English-language bookstore on the Left Bank is beloved by both locals and expats. Anglophone readers passing through Paris may come for the stock, but they stay to chat to Penelope, the charming owner, who'll pair you with a book you never knew you needed.

Street Style

Fancy heels and button-up shirts are mandates from yesteryear's Paris. Ditch the uniforms. Today, Parisians dress for comfort with a vintage flair of their own, mixing chic and casual, sporty and dressy.

SHINZO

Map 1; 23 Rue Étienne Marcel, 1st; ///hook.wink.kitchen; www.shinzo.paris/fr

The launch of a new brand of slick sneakers here is a notoriously big event: walk past on a trainer's national release day and you'll see a crowd of coolly clad sportswear aficionados lining up outside the store, eager to grab the latest offerings. From running shoes to

Shh!

Paris may be hot on *haute couture*, but you don't need to pay premium prices for designer gear. Skip the Champs-Élysées and head to the 6th instead for consignment store heaven. Chercheminippes *(www.cher cheminippes.fr)* is a hotspot for secondhand designer pieces like Louboutin bags and Jimmy Choo shoes – in great condition.

basketball footwear, this concept store covers every sports discipline, across four branches on the same road. Expect a suitably snazzy décor in each store: Shinzo are pros at the art of staging premium products, just stop by Shinzo Basketball to see their shrine to the NBA.

LESS IS MORE
Map 5; 22 Rue des Vinaigriers, 10th; ///harps.good.take; 09 52 70 87 60

The eco-conscious crowd swerve fast-fashion promoters and retreat to the comforting corners of this calming boutique, a stone's throw from Canal Saint-Martin. Owner Laetitia has shed all the frivolous packaging and only stocks items produced by eco-friendly manufacturers. You'll find a bit of everything: organic products, capsule collections, cute homewares. The vintage section, however, is the must-see area – bag one of the iconic blue work jumpsuits and you'll be the talk of the town.

FAGUO
Map 2; 81 Rue Vieille du Temple, 3rd; ///become.anchors.spice;
www.faguo-store.com/en

Glance down when you're strolling the streets of Paris and you'll probably spot someone wearing a pair of Faguo's tennis shoes – they're on the verge of becoming iconic. This carbon-positive brand is a favourite among millennials, who head here after work for a browse, knowing that for every item they purchase, this young and super-sustainable brand will plant a tree in a forest in France.

» Don't leave without buying a pair of shoes, distinguishable by the button sewn on the heel – they're France's answer to Converse.

ROUJE

Map 1; 11 bis Rue Bachaumont, 2nd; ///laser.round.brothers; https://fr.rouje.com

Imagine a charming Parisian flat bathed in warm lighting with refined flower arrangements, puffed-up sofas and nostalgic-looking photos adorning its walls. Well, wander over to Rue Bachaumont and you'll find this stylish paradise. Created by model-influencer Jeanne Damas, Rouje is one of the most *en vogue* local fashion dens. Join the young fashionistas in this pretty store to browse weekly releases of selected, innovative items and the occasional surprise capsule collection. One thing's for sure: you'll always find the French wardrobe essentials that 1970s icon Jane Birkin loved so dearly: think sober floaty dresses, old-school denim and chic it-girl bags.

» Don't leave without indulging in some delectable seasonal cuisine and fine wine (or good coffee if it's still a little early) at Chez Jeanne, the intimate bistro attached to Rouje.

KILIWATCH

Map 1; 64 Rue Tiquetonne, 2nd; ///take.bigger.crawled; www.kiliwatch-paris.com

Be prepared to trawl through 600 sq metres (6,400 sq ft) of quirky clothes at this cool-kid emporium. The vast size of this spot may seem a bit overwhelming at first but fear not, this is no ordinary vintage store: ready-to-wear collections are arranged by colour, style and type. Come the weekend, you'll see herds of hipsters hunting for a last-minute party outfit while vintage thrifters root through the rails for loud 1980s shirts, vintage Moschino and classic

A chic scarf is a cliché the French can't help but still embrace. Pick up a few at Kiliwatch and pay by the kilo.

Levi's denim. Whatever your style, it's probably here and though it's a tad pricey, it's worth it when you excavate a truly unique treasure.

MAD LORDS

Map 1; 316 Rue Saint-Honoré, 1st; ///warmers.rash.kebab; www.madlords.com

It's a bit of a treasure hunt finding this unisex jewellery store. Locate the wooden door, tucked away on a boutique-y street, and you'll be taken to a paved courtyard – on the other side of the courtyard lie the jewels. Shimmering from their displays, these heavy pieces are made for stacking and pairing with a couture leather jacket (à la Lenny Kravitz, who's a regular here). You'll have to have a fair bit of cash to splash if you're thinking of investing, but it's still a nice place to browse.

ISAKIN

Map 4; 9 Rue André del Sarte, 18th; ///curl.shampoo.spray; www.isakinparis.com

Thomas Traoré and his crew step up the Parisian street-style game with this exclusive "Made in Paris" brand. They preach comfortable, cool and sustainable menswear, primarily manufactured in local workshops with fabrics sourced from luxury upcycling. They've garnered a solid fanbase among urbanites, particularly for their best-selling graphic T-shirts (they're limited edition, so don't wait around).

Beauty Buys

"Make it simple and natural" is the ultimate motto for French beauty. Parisians maintain their ageless glow by tailoring their own perfect care routine from all the best products.

LIQUIDES BAR À PARFUM

Map 2; 9 Rue de Normandie, 3rd; ///trash.defended.sublet;
www.liquides-parfums.com

Parisians don't wait for the trends, they make them. This stylish shop's curated selection of little-known fragrances is like a cocktail bar for your nose (it even looks like a swanky drinks den inside). Just tell the person behind the counter what you're looking for, and they'll serve it up, even requiring you to wear a scent for a bit before

Try it!
SHAPE YOUR SCENT

Paris is practically the capital of perfume, so it's pretty mandatory to spend a couple of hours making your own at the Musée du Parfum's perfumer's workshop *(www.musee-parfum-paris.fragonard.com)*.

committing. Prices might be steep, but these long-lasting, quality products are worth it. Friends' eyes will roll when they ask where you got your fragrance and you say, "Oh, Paris," but you'll love it.

HUYGENS

Map 2; 24 Rue du Temple, 4th; ///openings.rush.ember; www.huygens.fr

A hit of lavender and eucalyptus arouse your senses upon stepping into this tiny boutique. Fittingly housed inside a former apothecary's home, Huygens is all about custom-made cosmetics. Take a whiff of each essential oil blend from the glass jars, then watch as the team infuses your choice into a soap or moisturizer. While you wait for your products, check out the cruelty-free candles, diffusers and other home aromatherapy goods that are proudly made in France – they're great for gifts (or just for spoiling yourself).

» Don't leave without buying a hand cream infused with the essential oils of your choice. Everyone needs a bit of luxury, right?

OH MY CREAM!

Map 1; 104 Rue du Bac, 7th; ///dusts.fire.stadium; www.ohmycream.com

If you feel the need to change up your routine but don't know where to start, let the super-friendly, well-informed counsellors at this beloved store guide you. You'll want to buy everything you set your eyes on, but the staff have an unparalleled knowledge and will only let you leave with products that suit your needs and skin type. There are no over-hyped products with unnecessary chemicals here; it's all about clean beauty and effective items from ethical brands.

NOSE

**Map 1; 20 Rue Bachaumont, 2nd; ///stripped.candy.index;
www.noseparis.com**

The name of this modern boutique says it all, really: let your sense
of smell guide you and you'll leave with your perfect scent. This
pretty apothecary-esque space takes perfumery all very seriously
with its personalized olfactory diagnoses. Locals rave about the fun
shopping experience, where you're encouraged to take a seat at the
fragrance bar (typically with a coffee) and get chatting to the expert
"noses" who question you on everything from your favourite smells
to what you expect from a perfume. What follows is a prescription
of sorts as the beauty experts trawl the shelves of branded bottles
to find a few scents that suit your tastes.Save yourself the fuss of
trailing around countless perfumeries and find that final invisible
touch to your Parisian style.

THE NAKED SHOP

**Map 3; 75 Rue Oberkampf, 11th; ///altering.lance.prompting;
www.thenakedshop.fr**

Packaging-free bulk cosmetics were nowhere to be found in the city
until this head-to-toe eco-friendly shop opened. Liquid goods like
shampoo, soaps and washing detergent are all sold by weight
thanks to self-service dispensers, which encourage you to bring your
own container or purchase a glass bottle that you can use time and
again (and even return for reimbursement). The palm-oil-free and
preservative-free products are all made in France, too, so whether
you're filling up with newcomer APO France or pioneer soaperie

Join the crowds and check out the discount sales at CityPharma for more bulk buys. It's worth it.

Marius Fabre, there's plenty to sweeten your bathroom aroma and conscience. Bulk-buying has never been so chic, and switching to zero waste never so easy.

L'OFFICINE UNIVERSELLE BULY

Map 1; 45 Rue de Saintonge, 3rd; ///sleeper.return.promote; www.buly1803.com

This trademark brand may be globally renowned, but the Marais boutique is one of a kind. It characterizes the charm of an area once inhabited by aristocrats, where dark wooden furniture, antique-style packaging and a replica of the 19th-century Grand Café Tortoni inside transport you to another era. The vintage products are the kind you'll want to keep even when empty to embellish your bathroom.

» **Don't leave without** buying a Superfin soap, which you can get customized with a golden vintage monogram, fit for royalty.

LOOX

Map 4; 15 Rue Vignon, 8th; ///research.bagels.shell; 01 87 16 99 88

Looking for the next big thing to add to your clean beauty cupboard? This minimalist concept store has you covered. Sure, you could stop in to restock your skincare supplies with classics from Dermalogica, but it's much more fun to pop caps on testers of French Girl body oils or sample a spritz of an unusual scent like Tobali's Smoke Flower. Many of the products are vegan and cruelty-free, so other than denting your bank balance, there's no need to feel guilty about a splurge.

BOULEVARD DE COURCELLES

Rifle through
VALOIS VINTAGE

Indulge a serious label obsession at this second-hand store, where a few hundred euros might snag you a pair of Prada flats or some Celine sunglasses.

BLVD HAUSSMA

BLVD MALESHERBES

PLACE CHARLES DE GAULLE

AVENUE DE FRIEDLAND

AVENUE

DES CHAMPS ÉLYSÉES

8TH

AVE MATIGNON

3

RUE DE SURÈNE

PLACE DE LA MADELE

Pay homage at
MUSÉE YVES
SAINT LAURENT

Walk the halls of the chic atelier where YSL designed his collections from 1974 to 2002, now a museum covering his life and work.

1

AVE MONTAIGNE

2

Window-shop along
AVENUE MONTAIGNE

Take a stroll down the glitziest avenue in Paris, pausing at Chanel, Givenchy and Dior.

PLACE DE LA CONCORDE

AVE DE PRÉSIDENT WILSON

AVE MONTAIGNE

16TH

La Seine

The Flame of Liberty, an unofficial memorial to Princess Diana, stands near **Pont d'Alma,** *where the fashion icon died in 1997.*

BLVD DE LA TOUR MAUBOURG

INVALIDES

7TH

BOULEVARD

AVENUE DE SUFFREN

BOULEVARD DES INVALIDES

BOULEVARD

0 metres   500
0 yards   500

AVENUE DE SÉGUR

An afternoon of
haute couture

Paris is considered the world's fashion capital for a reason. French style is synonymous with household names (Chanel, Dior, Louis Vuitton), but beyond these international juggernauts, there's so much more — not least the artists whose labels only later became runway staples. Avoid the Champs-Élysées proper — now the domain of chain shops and fast-food joints — and explore the surrounding streets, where consignment stores hold designer pieces at a fraction of the price and shops elevate clothing into a fine art.

Become an artisan at L'ÉCOLE DES ARTS JOAILLIERS
Book a hands-on, two-hour introduction to enamelling techniques at Van Cleef & Arpels' prestigious jewellery school.

PLACE VENDÔME

RUE D. CASANOVA

AVE DE L'OPÉRA

2ND

4

DE RIVOLI

ST

The arcades of the **Palais Royal** *have been the perfect runway setting for fashion-week shows from the likes of Louis Vuitton.*

GERMAIN

6TH

1. Musée Yves Saint Laurent
5 Avenue Marceau, 16th; www.museeyslparis.com
///helm.square.wishing

2. Avenue Montaigne
Avenue Montaigne, 8th
///masters.large.nibbles

3. Valois Vintage
8 Rue des Saussaies, 8th; www.valois vintage-paris.com
///mashing.nurse.touchy

4. L'École des Arts Joailliers
31 Rue Danielle Casanova, 1st; www.le colevancleefarpels.com
///vampire.coached.simply

 Pont d'Alma ///modes. zips.obstruction

Palais Royal ///smoking. copycat.caller

ARTS & CULTURE

Paris is shaped by its cultural landscape, which honours the masters of the past, admires the innovators of today and inspires the change-makers of tomorrow.

Museum Lates

Let tour groups, school children and chattering families take over the museums during the day. At night, these hubs belong to the locals, who get a post-work culture fix with the odd concert thrown in.

MUSÉE DU LUXEMBOURG

Map 1; 19 Rue de Vaugirard, 6th; ///moves.tumble.flexed; www.museeduluxembourg.fr

Often overlooked by out-of-towners, this museum is highly revered by locals – most of whom drop by for a quiet, pre-dinner culture fix on Monday evenings. There are only two exhibitions a year, often on leading figures from the art world, so check ahead and plan your trip well in advance if you have a preference for your art and artists.

CENTRE POMPIDOU

Map 2; Place George Pompidou, 4th; ///ignites.cones.words; www.centrepompidou.fr

Nights at this contemporary art centre belong to a young after-work crowd, all of whom know that when the industrial exterior lights up, the fun is just starting. Every week sees something new grace the calendar, whether it's a film screening or a dance show. Once the

When the Georges closes, head to nearby cosy bar Le Workshop, open until 2am, for a final glass of wine.

galleries close, those in the know take the escalator up to the rooftop Restaurant Georges, where post-gallery snacks and city views continue until midnight.

MUSÉE D'ORSAY

Map 1; 1 Rue de la Légion d'Honneur, 7th; ///pouch.ensemble.flames; www.musee-orsay.fr/fr

While this museum is flooded with narrating guides in the day, it's as still as a scene from a Monet painting on Thursday nights, when a sophisticated crowd peter in for evening concerts in the nave or intimate recitals in the auditorium. Instrumental crescendos make a stroll through the Impressionist art galleries all the more romantic.

» Don't leave without getting the perfect shot of Paris from above through the clock face on the fifth floor, with views over the Seine.

CITÉ DE L'ARCHITECTURE ET DU PATRIMOINE

Map 6; 1 Place du Trocadéro et du 11 Novembre, 16th; ///pricier.demand.forgets; www.citedelarchitecture.fr

Parisians are pretty into their architecture – unsurprising given how photogenic many of the city's buildings are. This spot charts the development of French architecture, and locals know there's no better time to visit than on Thursday nights, when they can end their evening with a fittingly dramatic view. From the upper floors you can see the Eiffel Tower lit up against the dark sky.

PALAIS DE TOKYO

Map 6; 13 Avenue du Président Wilson, 16th; ///connects.chambers.wiser; www.palaisdetokyo.com

You'll rarely see a painting in the concrete-clad exhibition spaces here. Instead, there's a heavy focus on multimedia and sensory installations, and works are often confrontational. A young, free-thinking crowd ponder the programme at the nightly openings, when a roster of boundary-pushing concerts, performances and screenings often come with a party vibe until midnight.

MUSÉE DU LOUVRE

Map 1; Pyramide du Louvre, Place du Carrousel, 1st; ///impulse.montage.cultivation; www.louvre.fr

Embark on one evening visit to the Louvre and, like any true Parisian, you'll never go in the daytime again. While that has a lot to do with the lack of giggling school groups and selfie-takers, it's also more

Shh!

The Louvre may be huge, but it's famously hard to find a quiet corner here during the day. Plus, even if you manage to glimpse the *Mona Lisa*, let's be honest: it'll likely only be through someone's smartphone.

Yet it is possible to escape the crowds within the heart of the world's most-visited museum: go upstairs to the Northern European painters or to the wings housing Islamic art, where tourists groups rarely go.

atmospheric at night, when a whole other world under the museum comes alive with concerts and lectures on art history. It's the live music that mostly draws in the post-work crowds, with international chamber music on Wednesday nights and more classic performances on Friday – just turn up by 7pm before the ticket office closes and enjoy.

» Don't leave without taking in the night lighting of I M Pei's famous pyramid outside, which seems dull during the day by contrast.

PALAIS GALLIERA
Map 6; 10 Avenue Pierre 1er de Serbie, 16th;
///caked.gangway.remodel; www.palaisgalliera.paris.fr

There's always a buzz in the air when this fashion museum opens its doors. It only stages two exhibitions a year, showcasing part of its 200,000-piece collection of clothing and accessories. As a result, attending an exhibit is an exclusive event, made all the more special on Thursday nights, when it stays open until 9pm. Budding designers and fashion students don their best outfits and trawl the halls of this Beaux-Arts palace, while the sun sets outside the bay windows.

MUSÉE DES ARTS ET MÉTIERS
Map 2; 60 Rue Réamur, 3rd; ///mint.drew.struts; www.arts-et-metiers.net

This underrated museum tempts end-of-the-week revellers inside with free admission after 6pm on a Friday, and the expansive collection of century-old bicycles and other curious gizmos makes them stay until closing at 9pm. It's set in the remains of an old priory, and the contrast between science and religion is lost on few who wander its halls.

Modern Art

Paris has always led the trends when it comes to art (Monet and Dalí, anyone?), and the city continues to shake up the scene today. Contemporary works make their way into vibrant spaces that rival the Louvre.

GALERIE PERROTIN

Map 2; 76 Rue de Turenne, 3rd; ///havens.cinemas.hill; www.perrotin.com

This international gallery is one for serious modern art fans. It rarely makes its way onto the tourist roster, rather attracting collectors and visitors from Hong Kong and New York (where some of Perrotin's other galleries are to be found). They all come to ponder exhibits by rising artists as well as big names like Takashi Murakami. It may be prestigious, but you won't feel out of place if you're not an art critic.

59 RIVOLI

Map 1; 59 Rue de Rivoli, 1st; ///digress.stewing.belong; www.59rivoli.org

The city's original art squat still feels counter-cultural, its quirky façade wedged amid the shops on commercial Rue de Rivoli. Now a colourful gallery (think art scribbled on each stairwell and stacked canvases teetering in each room) with working studios, 59 Rivoli is an inclusive space where free-thinking artists create away while chatting to the

A new exhibition is held on the ground floor every fortnight, so check the website to see what's on.

artsy Parisians who watch them at work. Come the weekend, revellers pack out every inch of the space for free musical concerts and performances.

LE BAL

Map 4; 6 Impasee de la Défense, 18th;
///blue.reaction.pastime; www.le-bal.fr

This former dance hall turned small non-profit gallery is so acutely Parisian. Exhibitions here use photography, video and new media to focus on "multiple possible approaches to reality", so it gets pretty philosophical, but that's why it's unique. By hosting thought-provoking shows from young artists and regular talks to accompany them, Le Bal dares to do something different, and dares to do it well.

» Don't leave without visiting the café, one of the earliest in Paris to serve gourmet brews in a coffee shop setting.

HALLE SAINT-PIERRE

Map 4; 2 Rue Ronsard, 18th; ///sushi.october.cool; www.hallesaintpierre.org

Montmartre may have a touristy reputation when it comes to its art scene, but while out-of-towners browse the canvas-lined stalls in Place du Tertre, avant-garde arty types escape to this cultural centre for an antidote to the mainstream. Inside a former market hall at the foot of the Sacré-Coeur, you'll find creatives pouring over unconventional forms of art at their leisure before sharing their views on the exhibitions over an espresso in the café.

ATELIER DES LUMIÈRES

**Map 3; 38 Rue Saint-Maur, 11th; ///waitress.finders.newest;
www.atelier-lumieres.com**

Missing out on an exhibition at this ground-breaking digital art gallery is such a travesty that Parisians go into a frenzy to nab tickets months in advance. This cultural spot has revitalized the fine art scene and made it accessible to all walks of life – you won't find any light-filled galleries with static portraits here. Instead, your visit is on your terms, whether you want to lie on the floor to watch moving works of art projected onto the ceiling or stand in the centre of a room, transfixed by the colours beneath your feet that move to the beats of music.

FONDATION LOUIS VUITTON

**Map 6; 8 Avenue du Mahatma Gandhi, 16th; ///miles.spooked.invent;
www.fondationlouisvuitton.fr**

Though this striking building is tucked away in the bucolic Bois de Boulogne, it's no secret, rising above the trees like billowing sails. The space is dedicated to contemporary art (rather than Vuitton's

Try it!
PICK A PASTEL

Inspired to create your own masterpiece? Head to La Maison du Pastel (www. lamaisondupastel.com), the world's oldest pastel manufacturer, to stock up on some tools. It's only open on Thursday afternoons.

signature fashion) and the unconventional exhibitions demand as much attention as the exterior, drawing creatives who religiously trek from the centre of Paris to attend new openings.

» **Don't leave without** seeing the view of Paris's skyline from the rooftop terrace. It's a unique vantage you won't find elsewhere.

MAISON EUROPÉENNE DE LA PHOTOGRAPHIE

Map 2; 5/7 Rue de Fourcy, 4th; ///glue.chairs.fairway; www.mep-fr.org

There's no place for frivolousness at this house of photography. Budding photographers get a close-up look at black-and-white works by notable artists, couples stroll hand in hand past avant-garde portraits in delicate frames and intrigued visitors ponder fine art shots with their heads craned. It's a sacred and minimalist affair, where neutral walls let the photos speak for themselves.

FONDATION CARTIER POUR L'ART CONTEMPORAIN

Map 6; 261 Boulevard Raspail, 14th; ///miss.shelved.various; www.fondationcartier.com

Few private foundations are appreciated by Parisians due to the city's many accessible public collections, but this foundation for contemporary art bucks that trend. Progressive works by artists — many young and relatively unknown — from different backgrounds draw a similar mix of bloggers, trendy locals and inquisitive students, who drop in for the visionary temporary exhibitions.

Esoteric Collections

There are museums, and then there are museums. Paris has a host of quirky and oftentimes hyper-specific collections that will surprise and capture your attention (perhaps more than the **Mona Lisa***).*

MUSÉE DU QUAI BRANLY–JACQUES CHIRAC

Map 6; 37 Quai Branly, 7th; ///outfit.biggest.tonic; www.quaibranly.fr
Behind a distinctive vegetal façade created by the inventor of the vertical garden, Patrick Blanc, lies the least conventional of Paris's big museums. Many of the objects and artworks housed in the modern ethnographic collections – African instruments, Aztec statues and Gabonese masks – were first displayed in 18th-century cabinets of curiosities as treasures brought back from Africa, Asia, Oceania and the Americas during the colonial era. These days, the curation is rather more nuanced and many of the exhibitions are superb, tempting Parisians to flock to every opening. The focus today is on cultural connection and dialogue, but some activists are still calling for the return of artifacts to their original home – in 2021, some were, with 26 items returned to the Republic of Benin.

» **Don't leave without** ambling through the outside grounds, which offer ample thinking space after touring the museum's collections.

MUSÉE DES ARTS FORAINS

Map 6; 53 Avenue des Terroirs de France, 12th; ///skips.trip.listings;
www.arts-forains.com

Close your eyes and you can almost smell candyfloss wafting through
the air. Curious kids and kidults alike have a soft spot for this living
museum dedicated to fairground arts, where taking a spin on a
hundred-year-old carousel is enough reason to keep returning. Its
founder, Jean-Paul Favand, began collecting rare items such as
German swings and a Hooghuys organ in the 1970s before realizing
that Paris was missing a space where laughter reigned supreme (in
the midst of all the serious war museums). Actor-guides raise spirits
on requisite tours year-round, but the space truly comes alive at
Christmas, when families flock to enjoy it at their own pace and
watch the likes of magicians and puppeteers perform dreamlike
stories. This is the place you'll be telling friends about once home.

MUSÉE JACQUEMART-ANDRÉ

Map 4; 158 Boulevard Haussmann, 8th; ///piglet.juices.infuses;
www.musee-jacquemart-andre.com

You can almost imagine the lavish parties that were held within
this Parisian mansion as you walk inside. The former private home
is a time capsule filled with *objets d'art* – including oodles of 18th-
century paintings and sculptures – collected from around the world
by art lovers Edouard André and Nélie Jacquemart. It's a rare glimpse
into the life once lived by a wealthy couple, where the grand staircase
and winter garden will leave you looking up real estate costs to see
if your budget could get you something similar in Paris.

MUSÉE DE L'ILLUSION

**Map 1; 98 Rue Saint-Denis, 1st; ///stews.tweeted.sounding;
www.museedelillusion.fr**

If your favourite museums are spaces of quiet contemplation, you might want to give this one a miss. Traditional curatorial rules – as well as the rules of gravity and space – are seemingly turned on their head here. Photo-taking is encouraged as you navigate upside-down rooms, discover the Beuchet Chair's mysterious powers and get dizzy in a "vortex tunnel". Come with friends or for a first date (though save the pints for after – it's psychedelic enough).

MUSÉE EDITH PIAF

Map 3; 5 Rue Crespin du Gast, 11th; ///because.ideas.ports; 01 43 55 52 72

Whether or not you've heard of the famed singer Edith Piaf, this little-known eccentric museum will make you feel like you know her intimately. Created by a lifelong fan, and requiring a phone call to

Shh!

Bet you never thought you'd find a museum dedicated to the simple pinball, right? Sure, you'll need to make an appointment in advance with owner Raphael to visit the secret Paris Pinball Museum *(www.pinball-gallery.com)*, but it's worth it. The collector has an impeccable knowledge of the history of pinball machinery and – even better – lets you play the vintage games for as long as you like.

enter, this tiny spot displays an expansive collection of painted portraits, private letters and a huge teddy bear owned by Piaf. It's all set inside an apartment once inhabited by the singer herself, so you can't help but feel like she'll appear in her little black dress.

MUSÉE DE MONTMARTRE

Map 4; 8–14 Rue Cortot, 18th; ///pardon.cookies.error;
www.museedemontmartre.fr

The walls of this former meeting place for artists echo with the voices of Renoir, Utrillo and Toulouse-Lautrec, whose works hang here today. Montmartre was once the heart of bohemian Paris, and nothing typifies that legacy quite like this vestige of the past, where you can imagine days fuelled by absinthe and finish with a view over the vines of Clos Montmartre that inspired the greats.

» Don't leave without visiting the faithfully restored atelier-apartment of renowned French painter Suzanne Valadon.

MUSÉE DE CLUNY

Map 2; 28 Rue du Sommerard, 5th; ///pizzas.intend.vets;
www.musee-moyenage.fr

A medieval treasure trove, housed in a Gothic mansion, built on Roman foundations – how's that for a holistic visit? If the architecture doesn't already impress, inside you can ogle the famed *Lady and the Unicorn* tapestries (said to be the *Mona Lisa* of the Middle Ages) and step down into Roman baths to learn about the city when it was just a little outpost called Lutetia.

On Stage and Screen

Paris's entertainment scene is driven by the characteristics that define the city: a passion for anti-conformism and a strong intellectual legacy. Kitsch musicals, gripping films and innovative dance await.

CINÉMA EN PLEIN AIR

Map 5; enter at 211 Avenue Jean Jaurès, 19th;
///vital.urban.sourced; www.lavillette.com

As long as the weather co-operates, the free outdoor screenings in the Parc de la Villette are the summer's biggest events, drawing young Parisians and families who aren't afraid to jostle for a spot on the lawn. Those seeking a touch of luxury rent lawn chairs, but most opt for a blanket on the grass. There's a European charm to it all: everyone cheers when the giant screen begins to inflate, and starts tucking into picnics as soon as the film starts.

CINÉ LE GRAND ACTION

Map 2; 5 Rue des Écoles, 5th; ///prefix.vipers.racks; www.legrandaction.com

The simplicity of the big red seats belie the intricate programming scheduled at this neighbourhood theatre. Despite the rise in popularity of Paris's multiplexes, this cinema continues a legacy of noteworthy retrospectives, ranging from independent films to Oscar-nominated pictures. It's a hub for true cinephiles, who come to debate at the film clubs and take notes at the industry talks on everything from the Cohen brothers to niche Japanese films.

ROCKY HORROR AT STUDIO GALANDE

Map 2; 42 Rue Galande, 5th; ///stage.kipper.crab; www.studiogalande.fr

The Rocky Horror Picture Show may be a worldwide phenomenon, but it's been so highly embraced by the French that letting loose at this unique mix of film and live action has become a rite of passage. The longest-running tribute to the cult movie has been bringing fans together since 1978 for a night of bold costumes, scandalous jokes and mayhem inside a tiny arthouse cinema. Parisians aren't outrageous very often, but all inhibitions are left at the door here, so come ready to dance and bring a bag of rice. (And make sure you book ahead.)

LE DIVAN DU MONDE

Map 4; 75 Rue des Martyrs, 18th; ///compounds.backs.modes; www.madamearthur.fr

This emblematic club remains under the radar to those who think Montmartre's cabaret scene starts and ends at the Moulin Rouge. Dance fanatics beg to differ, knowing the best show in town is put on by Madame Arthur, the troupe that have been performing cheeky spectacles and musical blind tests here since the 1940s.

» Don't leave without dancing into the early hours, long after your show has ended (performances run Thursday to Saturday).

Solo, Pair, Crowd

Whether you've got a day to yourself or are craving an entertaining night with your mates, there's a show to suit.

FLYING SOLO
Popcorn for one
One of the famous Latin Quarter cinemas, the tiny Ecoles Cinéma Club is the perfect place to cosy up and take in a nostalgic flick by yourself.

IN A PAIR
Broadway for besties
Get tickets to a musical at Théâtre Mogador on Rue de Mogador, which adapts crowd favourites, from *The Lion King* to *The Producers*, into French. It's a lot of fun.

FOR A CROWD
A screen for titans
Space isn't hard to come by at the sumptuous Grand Rex in the 2nd, also known as Europe's largest cinema theatre. Sit back and watch cinematic masterpieces play out on giant screens.

THÉÂTRE DU CHÂTELET

Map 1; 2 Rue Edouard Colonne, 1st; ///detained.owner.shave; www.chatelet.com

Anything staged here draws musical theatre lovers like moths to a flame. Fans come to see favourites like *42nd Street* performed in English, and keep returning in the hope of witnessing the next Tony Award winner (*An American in Paris* debuted here in 2014, after all).

LE LOUXOR

Map 4; 170 Boulevard de Magenta, 10th; ///bands.command.slime; www.cinemalouxor.fr

If the walls of this Egyptian Revival venue could talk, they would share stories of families watching movies in the 1920s and parties held by the gay community in the 1980s. After decades of abandonment, Le Louxor was restored to its cinematic glory in 2013 – much to the joy of those who visit as much for the history as for the indie films.

» Don't leave without enjoying an apéritif at the bar on the secret rooftop terrace before a cinema screening.

THÉÂTRE DE LA VILLE DE PARIS

Map 2; 2 Place du Châtelet, 4th; ///tingled.halt.promotes; www.theatredelaville-paris.com

The contemporary dance performed here is always cutting edge, drawing in creatives of a similar disposition. Sure, the modern auditorium is nothing special, but it's all about the innovative shows that have Parisians engaging in deep debates long after they finish.

City History

*Paris is a patchwork of groups and movements,
whose history is embedded in each arrondissement.
Whether it's evoking ancient history or immigrant
experiences, the city's past is always humbling.*

MUSÉE CARNAVALET

**Map 2; 23 Rue de Sévigné, 3rd; ///arrival.braked.watches;
www.carnavalet.paris.fr**

Tucked away in the Marais, this underrated museum is only visited by
those who know it's here. Spread across two mansions, the collection
traces the city's roots back to Neolithic cultures, through ancient
times and all the way to the Napoleonic era. It's an unparalleled
look at Parisian history, with toy guillotines and old street signs being
a few of the oddities to appreciate.

MUSÉE D'ART ET D'HISTOIRE
DU JUDAÏSME

Map 2; 71 Rue du Temple, 3rd; ///jaunts.fixated.games; www.mahj.org

It's fitting that a museum dedicated to Jewish culture and history in
France takes up space in the Marais, once the epicentre of the Jewish
community. Those seeking to learn about their heritage wander the

halls of this elegant mansion to see poignant photos one minute and an entire room dedicated to Hanukkah the next. Though the permanent collection is great, it's the thought-provoking talks and powerful temporary art exhibits that really draw inquisitive minds.

INSTITUT DU MONDE ARABE

Map 2; 1 Rue des Fossés Saint Bernard, 5th; ///crowbar.repair.display; www.imarabe.org

Many locals possess Arabic roots, but Paris was lacking a space that fostered the links between the Arab world and France until this cultural institute opened in the 1980s. Though tourists visit for its architecture – a contemporary build designed around the *mashrabiyya* – the interior draws a mixed crowd. Creatives trawl the Islamic art exhibits, academics bury themselves in tomes in the library and students book on to Arabic language courses.

» Don't leave without stopping for mint tea and Moroccan pancakes at the ground-floor café.

Shh!

Unbeknown to most locals, underneath Notre Dame lies an unsuspected vestige of ancient Paris – the Crypte Archeologique de l'Île de la Cité *(www.crypte.paris.fr)*. As you descend an unassuming stairwell in the plaza, you'll enter a crypt full of intact remains from over 2,000 years ago, which were found under the cathedral during renovations.

BLACK PARIS WALKS, LE PARIS NOIR

Map 2; Start at Place du Panthéon, 5th; ///also.sings.science;
www.leparisnoir.com

When Martinique-born Kévi Donat began to feel unsatisfied with the one-sided narrative told on Paris's walking tours, he set out to reveal the city's unspoken Black history on his own. What started for tourists quickly gained traction with a local crowd, no thanks to Kévi's knack for charismatic storytelling, an interactive way of touring (you won't be privy to a run of dull facts) and an infectious passion as he uncovers the roots of a Pan-African literary movement one minute and the legacy of slavery the next. Kévi's English-speaking walks are available privately, but you can't go wrong with his open tour. If you're interested in the intellectual and artistic side of Paris, take "The Pioneers of the Left Bank" and learn about the figures from the Caribbean, Africa and the USA who transformed this part of the city.

PANTHÉON

Map 2; Place du Panthéon, 5th; ///earliest.fallen.tall;
www.paris-pantheon.fr

Strolling through a mausoleum isn't for everyone, but this secular monument is intrinsic to the story of the French Revolution. Originally built as a church, it was transformed into a place to honour the great and the good of the Revolution era (and distinguished French citizens who came later). There's a mere six women buried here compared to 75 men, but in spite of its male bias, it's a fascinating place where locals come to feel inspired and humbled by their legacy. Intellectuals, politicians and historical figures are enshrined in the crypt below, so

To learn about the lesser-told history of women in Paris, take a walking tour with Women of Paris.

writer Victor Hugo and scientist Marie Curie aren't too far from your feet. If it all starts to feel too morbid, climb up to the dome for a panoramic view over the city.

MUSÉE NATIONALE DE L'HISTOIRE DE L'IMMIGRATION

Map 6; 293 Avenue Daumesnil, 12th; ///limp.unhappy.feelers; www.histoire-immigration.fr

Paris is a multicultural city, and this cultural centre devoted to immigration history lets locals comprehend their own identity and that of their country. The permanent exhibition, which sensitively depicts hardships and hopes, is reason enough to visit. But it's the donation gallery that strikes the most chords, with a resonating collection of personal objects and interview tapes that tell intimate stories.

MUSÉE RODIN

Map 6; 77 Rue de Varenne, 7th; ///humid.snares.tower; www.musee-rodin.fr

You can't think of Paris without appreciating its art history; in fact, you can't even visit the city without passing a museum dedicated to a pioneering artist. Of those museums, the former home and atelier of the founder of modern sculpture, Auguste Rodin, stands out. His legacy is felt in more than just the 300 works on display; it's in the gardens he fell in love with and the studio he sculpted in for nine years.

» Don't leave without seeing *The Thinker*, one of Rodin's most celebrated sculptures, amid the blooming roses in the garden.

Community Projects

Redefining the community centre are cool, urban spots taking up space in old buildings and abandoned stations. Places of refuge, these are somewhere all walks of life come together, and all voices are heard.

104 CENTQUATRE

Map 5; 5 Rue Curial, 19th; ///little.fraction.condiment; www.104.fr

This building may have once been the workplace for the city's undertakers (creepy, right?), but Parisians are breathing new life into it today. Creatives clear their minds with a relaxing Qi Gong class in the morning, budding painters pop in for chats with the artists in residence before taking a painting workshop, and energetic dancers use the open spaces to practise their new routines in front of passersby.

LA RECYCLERIE

Map 4; 83 Boulevard Orano, 18th; ///outreach.patting.chief; www.larecyclerie.com

Okay, there are chickens, so you know what you're getting into here. Everything at this former railway station is devoted to an eco-friendly ethos of reuse: an urban farm features a communal vegetable patch; seed swaps encourage community building; and a workshop lets people drop off items to be repaired in-house. Plus, if things are too broken to fix, the team find a way to give it new life – and teach you how to do it yourself next time. Zero waste may seem like a fantasy, but here, it's become a reality.

» Don't leave without visiting the café to grab a coffee for yourself and one for someone in need (there's a pay-it-foward scheme here).

LE SHAKIRAIL

Map 5; 72 Rue Riquet, 18th; ///exposing.feels.bundles;
www.shakirail.curry-vavart.com

You know you've arrived when you reach a seemingly abandoned house fronted by messy chairs and stacks of unidentified objects. No, this isn't a squat – it's a shelter for artistic vagabonds. This welcoming cultural centre is a hive of energy, where locals bond over a series of cool events – a ceramics workshop one day, a film screening the next.

Tucked away in the upscale 16th is Les Cinq Toits *(www. lescinqtoits.fr)*, a community space housed in an old police station. It's a chilled-out spot where you can come to take hands-on classes, like bike reparing and candle making.

The big, flag-decked yard is home to Le Récho's, a restaurant that trains and supports refugees (many of whom stay in the building's social accommodation), and which serves up platefuls of organic grub.

Liked by the locals

**"I've been going to La Mutinerie
since I was eighteen and I love it
to this day. It's always felt
comfortable, and somewhere
I belong as a lesbian."**

DALIA, ILLUSTRATOR

GROUND CONTROL

Map 6; 81 Rue du Charolais, 12th; ///juniors.calls.bill;
www.groundcontrolparis.com

This popular cultural centre gives off the feel of a mini village, housing all the requisites needed to practically move in. It's the kind of place where you can thrift shop in the afternoon, join a debate in the early evening and finish your day with a bite to eat from the food trucks.

» Don't leave without checking out the Ground boutique – half concept store, half cabinet of curiosities – for a unique gift.

LE HASARD LUDIQUE

Map 4; 128 Avenue de Saint Ouen, 18th; ///drain.starred.choppy;
www.lehasardludique.paris

Tattoo events, pub quizzes and *pétanque* matches are just a taste of the cool events at this communal hub. Thanks to a crowd-funding initiative set up by three young Parisians, a matching young clientele now enjoy a bar and concert hall inside this former train station.

LA MUTINERIE

Map 2; 176 Rue Saint-Martin, 3rd; ///leaned.crowbar.remover;
www.lamutinerie.eu

Anyone walking past La Mutinerie may assume it's simply a bar – but it's so much more. This multi-functional safe space brings the LGBTQ+ community together through regular support evenings, monthly tattoo events, self-defence classes and so much more. Better still, it frequently donates 10–15 per cent of turnover to the LGBTQ+ community.

Ponder paintings in
MUSÉE GUSTAVE
MOREAU

Wander through this symbolist painter's one-time family home, transformed into a museum by Moreau and filled with his artworks.

*The world's oldest pastel producer, **La Maison du Pastel** has been making Roché pastels since 1720, and on this site since 1906.*

Become acquainted at
59 RIVOLI

Climb a graffiti-covered spiral staircase to dip in and out of the 30 studios at this art squat. The permanent and transient residents are happy for you to watch them at work.

*Traders have been selling books and prints at the bouquinistes' stalls along the **Quai de l'Hôtel de Ville** for five centuries.*

9TH

10TH

RUE LA FAYETTE

BLVD HAUSSMANN

RUE MONTMARTRE

2ND

PLACE DE LA CONCORDE

1ST

RUE DU LOUVRE

La Seine

BLVD DE SÉBASTOPOL

3RD

BLVD BEAUMARCHAIS

MARAIS

RUE DE RIVOLI

4TH

PL. DE BAST

BOULEVARD ST-GERMAIN

6TH

BOULEVARD

RASPAIL

BOULEVARD ST-MICHEL

5TH

La Seine

BOULEVARD DE L'HÔPITAL

13TH

MONTPARNASSE

BOULEVARD MONTPARNASSE

14TH

BOULEVARD DE PORT-ROYAL

0 metres   800
0 yards   800

BELLEVILLE

**Get immersed at
ATELIER DES
LUMIÈRES**
Book a timed "showing"
and experience classical
paintings like never
before: animated and
set to music.

4

11TH

AVENUE PARMENTIER

R. FAIDHERBE

RUE CHALIGNY

12TH

AVENUE DAUMESNIL

BERCY

3

**Lunch at
GROUND
CONTROL**
Swing by this community-
space-meets-food-court
for some treats and to see
if a craft workshop is on.

An afternoon exploring
Paris's art scene

Art takes many forms in Paris. Centuries-old
masterpieces adorn the city's world-class
museums, while counter-cultural movements
make way for new, fresh talents — and all types
of art are met with the same level of awe and
admiration. This is a city where street art secretly
appears overnight, galleries show traditional
works in untraditional ways and single-artist
museums shed light on the personality as well as
artistry of great masters. Parisians love nothing
more than to span styles and eras, and debate
the intricacies of each, on a lazy afternoon.

1. Musée Gustave Moreau
14 Rue de la Rochefoucauld,
9th; www.musee-moreau.fr
///twisty.crystal.rubble

2. 59 Rivoli
59 Rue de Rivoli, 1st;
www.59rivoli.org
///digress.stewing.belong

3. Ground Control
81 Rue du Charolais,
12th; www.ground
controlparis.com
///juniors.calls.bill

4. Atelier des Lumières
38 Rue Saint-Maur, 11th;
www.atelier-lumieres.com
///waitress.finders.newest

La Maison du Pastel ///
tractor.even.palace

Quai de l'Hôtel de Ville
///compiled.sides.swinging

NIGHTLIFE

Paris's easy-going nature extends to its nightlife scene. Friends catch up over apéritifs, groups dance along the banks of the canal and musicians play in intimate venues.

Guinguettes and Rooftops

Drinking outdoors is a Parisian pastime, and one that gets all the more ritualistic on balmy summer nights. As soon as night falls, locals battle for spots on rooftops and at open-air café-bars.

LE PERCHOIR MÉNILMONTANT

Map 3; 14 Rue Crespin du Gast, 11th; ///browser.relate.loaf; www.leperchoir.fr

The Perchoir group may expand their terrace empire each year, but if you hear talk of a "Le Perchoir" in passing, this is the one. It's the place to see and be seen, where trendy locals come to pose on low bed-style benches, rate everyone's best summer outfits and sip cocktails while overlooking the city's rooftops as the sun goes down.

ROSA BONHEUR

Map 5; Parc des Buttes-Chaumont, 2 Avenue de la Cascade, 19th; ///nuzzled.toggle.healers; www.rosabonheur.fr

Tucked inside Parc des Buttes-Chaumont's easternmost entrance, this idyllic *guinguette* (open-air café/bar) is a summer "it" spot. On Sundays, it turns into an unofficial LGBTQ+ bar (its namesake, the

Get here really early – like 3pm early – on Sundays to avoid having to wait in the famously long queues.

realist painter Rosa Bonheur, was a lesbian). Expect romance blossoming over bottles of rosé (they pretty much dot every table) and a dance to a pop tune or two.

PÉNICHE MARCOUNET

Map 2; Port des Célestins, Quai de l'Hôtel de Ville, 4th;
///proud.dangerously.divided; www.peniche-marcounet.fr

Forget about those Paris movie clichés for a moment: you really can dance to jazz on the banks of the Seine. Instead of couples in 1920s-style frocks and penguin suits, though, picture easy-going crowds perched at wooden pallet tables, drinking beers and sharing plates of BBQ grub, before swaying to sultry tunes. That's the exact scene you'll get when you come to this barge bar between May and October.

MAMA SHELTER EAST

Map 6; 109 Rue de Bagnolet, 20th; ///volunteered.riches.snoring;
www.mamashelter.com

It's locals rather than hotel guests who take over this semi-secret rooftop on sunny nights. Hours pass in the blink of an eye beneath candy-coloured parasols, with the help of regular rosé top-ups and a pizza or two brought up from the ground-floor pizzeria. The views aren't the best in town, but you'll be having too much fun to notice.

» Don't leave without challenging a stranger to a game of ping pong to reveal your competitive side.

Solo, Pair, Crowd

Nothing captures the romance of Paris like gazing out over the city's rooftops with a cocktail in hand.

FLYING SOLO
Artistic tendencies
After checking out the latest exhibition at the Centre Pompidou *(p108)*, splurge on a glass of champagne at Le Georges, the centre's striking rooftop bar-restaurant.

IN A PAIR
Get high
The views from the Terrass" Hotel's rooftop bar will stop you in your tracks: you can see almost the entire city spread out around the Eiffel Tower from this Montmartre hotel. It's the perfect backdrop for a catch-up.

FOR A CROWD
Time to dine
Book a large table at the rooftop bar Brasserie Auteuil in the 16th for pizza and limoncello spritzes, surrounded by a lush green jungle of towering plants.

PAVILLON PUEBLA

**Map 5; Parc des Buttes-Chaumont, 39 Avenue Simon Bolivar, 19th;
///milder.juggler.wicked; www.leperchoir.fr**

A patio doubles as a cocktail bar with a dance floor at this fairy-light-lit cabin, nestled in the southernmost tip of Parc des Buttes-Chaumont. It feels like you've rocked up to a laid-back house party, thanks to the mismatched seating and pop playlist.

LE TOP DU POINT EPHÉMÈRE

**Map 5; 200 Quai de Valmy, 10th; ///bunny.enforced.remover;
www.pointephemere.org**

When locals pass this bar and concert venue in the summer, they're on the lookout for one thing: a green flag hanging outside, signalling the opening of the trendy rooftop terrace. It's a laidback spot where a fun young crowd linger for hours on beach chairs, watching the sun set over the Canal Saint-Martin while sipping on a beer.

» Don't leave without checking the venue's schedule while you're here. You might be able to catch drag bingo or a vintage market inside.

LA JAVELLE

**Map 6; entrance facing 20 Boulevard Poniatowski, 12th;
///quiz.indirect.added; www.lajavelle.com**

This summer *guinguette* may have moved from west to east, but it remains as popular as ever thanks to a village-fair vibe. It's a little eclectic: expect yoga lessons and recycling workshops during the day, and lively music and dancing once the sun goes down.

Music Nights

Banish any preconceived ideas of a pretentious music scene in the French capital. Sure, live jazz has its place, but vinyl-only DJ sets and underground metal gigs tempt Parisians to dance until the early hours.

LA SEINE MUSICALE

Map 6; Île Seguin, Boulogne-Billancourt; ///minds.decide.eyebrows; www.laseinemusicale.com

It takes a strikingly modern concert hall of this calibre to persuade the busiest of Parisians to venture to a small island in the Seine. An approach to making orchestral music accessible to all walks of life attracts more than the average opera crowd here, where even non-ticket-holders can appreciate the fantastic acoustics and choir performances going on inside from the big screen outside the venue.

LA BELLEVILLOISE

Map 5; 19–21 Rue Boyer, 20th; ///dressy.gateway.cherry; www.labellevilloise.com

Only in Paris can a venue span an exhibition space, cultural hub and club with ease. This spot is always a safe bet for a memorable night out, whether you're settling in on one of the wooden chairs to

Book a table for the famed Sunday jazz brunch. It's great for large groups, with heaps of good food.

listen to a live acoustic set after work or letting loose to a DJ spinning Latin American cumbia rhythms and hip-hop tunes on Friday and Saturday nights.

LE MAZETTE

Map 6; 69 Port de la Rapée, 12th; ///extremes.speared.luring; 01 43 45 67 67

Taking over the mooring once held by the legendary floating club Concrete, this barge venue has brought a lighter vibe to the *quais*. Teetering on the edge of both bar and club, it attracts a mixed crowd who party to varied line-ups on three sprawling floors. With disco DJ sets and stand-up-and-sing-with-the-band karaoke, you'll find yourself returning several nights in a row along with the locals.

» Don't leave without checking out the photogenic rooftop deck, complete with strings of fairy lights and its own bar.

SUPERSONIC

Map 3; 9 Rue Biscornet, 12th; ///hatter.sting.slide; www.supersonic-club.fr

The rock and indie scene is very much alive and well at this industrial, multi-floor club. Any tune with a guitar solo goes down well with the energetic crowd, who get more raucous as the night wears on – expect a splash of beer or two from a bopping neighbour while the floor vibrates with music. Some big names cross the threshold, but Supersonic also keep things grounded with themed genre nights. Many of the gigs are free before 11pm, but you'll need plenty of stamina to stay till close (6am) like the rest of them.

LA GARE

Map 5; 1 Avenue Corentin Cariou, 19th; ///residual.cooks.ripe

In-the-know crowds trek quietly to the outer edges of the 19th for free jazz gigs and electro nights here, where word-of-mouth draws in the cool kids in the absence of a website and landline. This standing-room-only and graffiti-scrawled venue – once a train station – may be a laidback spot with cheap beers, but absolute silence and respect is enforced for the artists. Between sets, everyone pours out onto the forecourt to chat and smoke before being shh-d as they cram back in.

CIRQUE ELECTRIQUE

Map 6; Place du Maquis du Vercors, 20th; ///portable.crown.region;
https://cirque-electrique.com

A patch of concrete above a ring road might seem an odd location for one of Paris's most avant-garde venues, yet it works. That's because once you step inside this circus-themed complex – which

The plain grey front door of Le Klub *(www.leklub-paris.com)* belies the frenetic energy that greets you once you're inside. Tucked away in the 1st, this spot is one of the best venues in Paris for head-banging rock music, whether it's punk or psychedelic, new-wave or metal. As you'd suspect from the name, it also hosts club nights, too, with DJ sets that rock the venue from 12am until dawn.

comes complete with a couple of big top tents – the outside world melts away. Cabaret, burlesque and circus performances are all part of the show here, but it's the live music that really steals the spotlight. Expect an eclectic mix of genres, including post-punk, screamo and rock-and-roll; there's even a bit of classical on offer.

ÉGLISE ST SULPICE

Map 1; 2 Rue Palatine, 6th; ///unhappy.guard.boater; www.classictic.com

Paris's churches all start to blend together, but an organ recital or concert at this nearly regal church – the city's second-largest house of worship – will be memorable. It's a rite of passage for families to attend holiday concerts here, but you don't need to wait until Christmas to hear the pipes do their thing. Simply book ahead for one of the classical evening concerts and settle into the church pews; the impressive acoustics and stained-glass windows make for a spellbinding treat.

PHILHARMONIE DE PARIS

Map 5; 221 Avenue Jean Jaurès, 19th; ///qualified.chilling.creeps; www.philharmoniedeparis.fr

Don't spend too long debating the controversial, glitzy spaceship-like exterior of this concert hall: it's all about the music and the modern acoustic technology once you're inside. The futuristic theatre itself features innovative seating, so there's no bad spot in the house from which to enjoy a bit of live jazz or a symphony performance.

» Don't leave without checking out the museum, which tends to host special exhibits dedicated to musical figures and greats.

Game Night

Gaming culture flies under the radar in Paris, but it's surprisingly strong. Whether you have a penchant for board games or fancy trying your hand at pétanque, there's always a playground for the young at heart.

CHEZ BOUBOULE

Map 3; 26 Avenue Jean Aicard, 11th; ///faster.players.share; www.chezbouboule.fr

One of three spots to share the same name and concept, this indoor *pétanque* bar is party central at the weekend, when you can hardly see or hear the matches in action over the chatter and music. Bring a group of friends, get here early and chalk your names on the wall to secure a slot on the pitch. You don't need your own set of balls, but

Try it!
PLAY PÉTANQUE

Once you've mastered the French art of *pétanque*, take it outdoors. Games on the terrains backing the Quai de la Loire *(p148)* tend to be relaxed, while more serious matches go on late along Rue Botzaris.

you will need a grasp of the rules: getting your boules as close as possible to the jack. Knocking your opponents out of the way is encouraged, as is sipping on a Lillet and tonic as you strategize.

RESET

Map 1; 17 Rue du Cygne, 1st; ///deserved.handbag.scout; www.reset.bar

Stroll a few minutes through the bar-filled backstreets north of Châtelet and you'll stumble across this time machine, ready to transport you back to childhood. At this bar-meets-video-game paradise, a raft of classic arcade and console games have been brought back to life. The screens are the décor here, and Atari, Street Fighter II and early Nintendo 64 smash-hits like Goldeneye 007 are just the start of the retro mania. Everyone from square-eyed gamers to daters in search of a nostalgic night out come to find their own slice of fun.

» Don't leave without ordering a sweet and creamy Bomberman cocktail with rum, amaretto, cream, vanilla and cinnamon. Think of it as a (grown-up) throwback to a milkshake.

LE BAR À PINTES

Map 3; 111 Rue Saint-Maur, 11th; ///letter.shins.stewing; www.lebap.fr

Proper dive bars are hard to come by in Paris, and bars with pool tables even more so, which makes this sometimes rowdy spot, signed as "Le BAP" from the street, worth seeking out. It's opted for a French spin on Americana, so expect references to *baby-foot* and billiards rather than foosball and pool. The generous happy hour prices will give you the confidence to challenge strangers to a game or two.

GAMELLE

Map 3; 29 Avenue Daumesnil, 12th; ///protest.salutes.refrain;
www.gamelle-paris.fr

You'd be forgiven for thinking Gamelle is just a regular bar from the
crowds drinking outside. But elbow your way through and you'll enter
a loft-style hangout, where a mini bowling lane, pinball tables and a
dart board await you and your most competitive friends. Sipping on
a Gin To' Gamelle – Gamelle's signature gin and tonic with fresh
mint and cinnamon – is pretty mandatory between turns.

GOSSIMA PING PONG BAR

Map 3; 4 Rue Victor Gelez, 11th; ///homing.agreeing.verse; www.gossima.fr

Ping pong and pints make for the perfect combination at this bar,
where nights are set to the echo of balls flying on and off the tables
(and occasionally the walls). Good tunes and great cheese boards
make this a popular party venue, but plenty of friends also stop by for
a little one-on-one competition still suited from the office early in the
evening. Eight tables are spread across two sparsely decorated
floors and a private room, so book ahead to get a table.

À LA FOLIE PARIS

Map 5; Parc de la Villette, 19th; ///ramming.correct.pylons;
www.alafolie.paris

It's all fun and games at this self-styled *néo-guinguette* out in the Parc
de La Villette, one of the few parks where only Parisians tend to tread.
It's a bit of an indoor-outdoor playground that welcomes anyone up

for a good time. In summer, that means rounds of Mölkky (Finnish skittles) between sips of drinks at picnic tables; in winter, expect raucous games of drag bingo (one of few drag events in Paris) indoors.

LE DERNIER BAR AVANT LA FIN DU MONDE

Map 1; 19 Avenue Victoria, 1st; ///obeyed.juices.lodge; www.dernierbar.com
You'll roam from steampunk to Star Destroyer on the different levels of this geek enclave, where devoted Parisians huddle over board games with a drink for company. Grab a beer, choose from the vast selection of games – in all states of pre-loved distress – and settle in. It's a haven for sci-fi fans, so you might want to prepare a *Star Wars* or *Lord of the Rings* reference to impress the regulars (though if you're heading here already, you probably don't need coaching).
>> Don't leave without grabbing a refreshing C3PO fruit mocktail infused with vanilla. You need your wits to win, right?

BOWLING DE PARIS FRONT DE SEINE

Map 6; 15 Rue Gaston de Caillavet, 15th; ///puddles.uptake.speak;
www.xbowlingsympas.com
Sure, Parisians are more known for schooling opponents over a game of *pétanque* than a round of bowling, but these lanes, connected to a swanky shopping mall, teem with locals nonetheless. Drumming up memories of birthday parties and first dates, this beloved hall draws groups of friends and families with kids in tow every night of the week, all looking for an excuse to let loose after work and school.

Open-air Living Rooms

When the sun goes down, Parisians refuse to go home. Every inch of the city's streets become communal backyards after dark, with locals gathering to drink, socialize and dance outdoors.

QUAI DE LA LOIRE

Map 5; Quai de la Loire, 19th; ///husbands.pinch.gifts

This broad, calm canal is a local alternative to the Seine – and with more action. Parisians use its wide banks for *pétanque* matches, which start late in the day and continue into the evening. Bring your own set and stake out a spot; if you haven't packed these heavy metal balls, the nearby BarOurcq usually rents out sets for those lucky enough to get there before they're gone.

CANAL SAINT-MARTIN

Map 5; Canal Saint-Martin, 10th; ///towns.requested.ketchup

The din of evening revellers can be heard as you approach this hotspot. Students and edgy locals mingle late into the night here, cradling a few beers and tucking into hummus from the local

Order a pizza at Pink Flamingo and find a spot on the quay – they'll bring your food over to you.

grocery store as they occupy every last centimetre of space along the canal. On hot summer evenings, the most daring jump from the iron bridges to cool off.

PARC DU CHAMP-DE-MARS

Map 6; enter at Avenue Joseph Bouvard; ///october.truck.menu

This is one is so obvious that we almost forget to mention it. Running from the Eiffel Tower to the École Militaire, this long stretch of lush lawn is perfect for an evening picnic come summer. Avoid the end closest to the Iron Lady (unsurprisingly, it's where camera-toting tourists congregate) and make for the southeast section instead. Here, as homeward-bound families round up their kids and students uncork bottles of wine, spread out your blanket and settle in (the park's open 24 hours), watching as the Eiffel Tower puts on a sparkly show every hour.

PLACE DU MARCHÉ SAINTE-CATHERINE

Map 2; Place du Marché Sainte-Catherine, 4th; ///crew.mutual.uptake

While out-of-towners overlook this little leafy square in favour of nearby Place des Vosges, locals take advantage of the space here, chatting on the benches over a pitcher of wine from one of the cafés that line the plaza. It becomes one big communal terrace at night, when impromptu musicians fill the air with lively tunes and the laughter and conversation carry on till late.

» Don't leave without getting a glass of rosé from Chez Joséphine around the square's edge to enjoy while the sun sets.

PONT DES ARTS

Map 1; Pont des Arts, 6th; ///grades.wipes.airless

This bridge practically doubles as a giant couch. Lovers gazing at the sunset, an artist painting a landscape on an easel, a busker strumming a song – those Paris clichés are all here. The romantic edge dates back to the time when clunky rusty metal padlocks gave this bridge the nickname "love lock bridge"; though the locks have gone, it's still a charming place to bring a bottle of bubbly, take a seat against the railings and sip the night away.

JARDIN TINO-ROSSI

Map 2; 2 Quai Saint-Bernard, 5th; ///vitals.trams.sleep

There's nothing dreamier than dancing on the banks of the Seine on a balmy Parisian night. During the summer, cha-cha, hip-hop and ballet sessions are a regular sight in the small amphitheatres along this riverside park, but it's the tango dancing that draws most locals.

Shh!

Tango dancing on the Seine may be a popular event in the summer, but those that dread coming unprepared head to the riverbank at 7pm – an hour and a half before the performances start – for a free tango lesson. They're held by Tango Argentin, the friendly organizers of the dancing event at Jardin Tino-Rossi, from Wednesday to Sunday, June through September. Simply turn up with a pair of comfy shoes.

Ladies bring their dancing shoes, skirts catch in the breeze and things heat up until midnight. Don't have a partner? Someone will pick you out of the crowd, so prepare to swing and dip (or gracefully decline from the sidelines). Audrey Hepburn would totally approve.

» Don't leave without exploring the Musée de la Sculpture en Plein Air, where you'll find sculptures by the likes of Ossip Zadkine.

JARDIN DU CARROUSEL
Map 1; Place du Carrousel, 1st; ///fest.slacker.sifts

The grassy gardens directly in front of the Louvre are far from a secret, but unknown to out-of-towners is the fact that they're open all night. Friends come for post-work wind-downs, stretching out with a blanket and nibbling on a baguette while the odd frisbee gets their attention flying overhead. It doesn't get more Parisian than seeing the Eiffel Tower illuminated in the distance and the palatial museum sitting behind you.

JARDIN NELSON MANDELA
Map 1; 1 Place du René Cassin, 1st; ///dude.beefed.rust

When you spot the giant statue of a head, you've arrived. Known to locals as Jardin Les Halles, the area in the shadows of St Eustache church has had a facelift in recent years, with heaps of seating added that make it more amenable to hanging out than ever before. By day, parents watch their kids in the playground, but by night, the green space becomes the domain for friends catching up before heading off to the nearby Marais.

Apéritif Spots

*A quick pre-dinner apéritif (or **apéro**) is a sacred tradition in Paris, marking the transition from day to night. When work days end, it's straight to a bar where fuss and reservations are not on the menu.*

AGROLOGY

Map 3; 15 Rue de Prague, 12th;
///rails.homework.december; www.agrology.fr

At a glance you could easily mistake Agrology for a wine shop and grocery store, but there's just enough space for a few start-of-evening drinks – either inside or on a pavement table in good weather. The bottle selection has a Mediterranean leaning, with plenty of wines from beyond France's borders: a welcome change when many *apéro* hours mean a choice between Beaujolais, Bordeaux and Chablis.

LE LABO

Map 1; 37 Rue des Lombards, 1st; ///surviving.frantic.bounty;
www.thelabo.fr

There's always high energy at this LGBTQ+ haven, where students, couples and trendy folk spill out onto the pavement terrace with cheap drinks. There are lots of gay bars in the area, but Le Labo is notably larger and more welcoming to all genders, sexes and sexualities, so it's the spot of choice for those seeking a quick drink in a friendly atmosphere. Pop in for happy hour on Tuesday, when drinks are even cheaper, the crowd rowdier and intimate conversations a no-go.

CAFÉ DU COIN

Map 3; 9 Rue Camille Desmoulins, 11th; ///fellow.inserted.blaring; 01 48 04 82 46

When you find a café that opens at 8am for locals to drink espresso bleary-eyed at the bar, then stays busy all the way through to 2am most nights a week, you know you're onto a good thing. Though the affordable lunchtime *formules* draw office workers weekly, it's the always heaving *apéro* that people tell their colleagues about. Meet your friends early to sate your pre-dinner hunger with a pizzette and a glass of natural wine to see what all the fuss is about.

» Don't leave without trying the seemingly simplest (but tastiest) pizzette of the day, usually topped with mozzarella, ham and harissa.

PIGNON

Map 4; 9 Rue Brochant, 17th; ///senses.apron.publish

It's easy to see why the 17th is increasingly being hailed one of the city's coolest quartiers when you stop for a drink at Pignon. It's the kind of place where friends meet after work to sip on bottles of Parisian-brewed beer, tuck into sharing plates and shout over a few games of table football before wandering onwards in search of dinner. In short: a casual spot to get a taste of the Batignolles bar scene.

LE PETIT FER Á CHEVAL

Map 2; 30 Rue Vieille du Temple, 4th; ///bridge.waffle.horses;
www.cafeine.com/petit-fer-a-cheval

This traditional café-bistro is one of renowned Marais restaurateur Xavier Denamur's clutch of addresses, so it's a bit of an institution. It's a tiny spot, and the pavement tables are too small to comfortably settle into for long, but this makes it the perfect place to drop by for a quick glass of rosé before moving on.

CRAVAN

Map 6; 17 Rue Jean de la Fontaine, 16th; ///fend.verse.defended

The sleepy 16th was once the last place you'd go for a well-made drink, but thanks to Cravan, it's finally shaking off its reputation as a cocktail desert. Strong drinks served in elegant coupe glasses are the speciality here, so even one will get your night off to a storming start.

» Don't leave without trying The Tunnel, a sophisticated twist on a Negroni, with Noilly Prat, Campari and Punt E Mes, served straight.

LA FONTAINE

Map 5; 31–3 Rue Juliette Dodu, 10th; ///migrants.bucket.cobbles;
www.cafesbelleville.com

Once easily overlooked, this quintessential corner café is now reimagined in all but appearance. Set up a few blocks from the canal, it draws more locals and devotees than tourists for the creative cocktails and nibbles – great for a quick stop on your way to dinner or more drinks along the canal.

Liked by the locals

"*Apéro* is another reason to make eating and drinking last all night, rather than a few hours. It's an early happy hour with finger food and friends that gets you ready for a big meal."

BARBARA DONADELLO, EVENTS PLANNER

2ND

RUE ÉTIENNE MARCEL

RUE DE TURBIGO

**Get a culture fix at
MUSÉE DU LOUVRE**
Wander the halls before
close (6pm, unless it's a late
opening), and admire the
pyramid at golden hour.

3RD

1

1ST

QUAI F. MITTERAND

La Seine

QUAI DE LA
MÉGISSERIE

*Since 2019, the
renowned theatre and
opera house* **Théâtre
du Châtelet** *has been
home to a hidden night
club, Club Joséphine.*

2

Q. DE GESVRES

PLACE
DE L'HÔTEL
DE VILLE

MARAIS

RUE DE RIVOLI

4TH

**Bag a spot at
SQUARE DU
VERT-GALANT**
Dangle your feet above
the Seine at the western
end of Île de la Cité,
sharing an *apéro* while
the city lights sparkle.

*Île de
la Cité*

3

Q. DE CÉLESTINS

6TH

LATIN
QUARTER

**Sway to music at
PÉNICHE
MARCOUNET**
Catch a live jazz show on the
atmospheric terrace of this
péniche (barge) while tucking
into sharing plates of food.

*Île St-
Louis*

BLVD ST - GERMAIN

QUAI HENRY IV

La Seine

BOULEVARD ST - MICHEL

RUE ST - JACQUES

5TH

RUE
MONGE

QUAI ST - BERNARD

13TH

BOULEVARD DE L'HÔPITAL

0 metres 500
0 yards 500

An evening following
the Seine path

The Seine is as much at the heart of Paris after dark as it is during the day. On sunny evenings, it's Parisians, not visitors, that pack the *quais* to watch the sunset over the water. Nights out start late and continue at a relaxed pace, so you can catch an exhibition, stroll along the river, have an apéritif or two and only start to think about where you might dance the night away around 11pm. Parisians aren't generally big plan-makers when it comes to bar-hopping: just follow the river's calling and see where the evening takes you.

1. Musée du Louvre
Pyramide du Louvre, Place du Carrousel, 1st; www.louvre.fr
///impulse.montage.cultivation

2. Square du Vert-Galant
15 Place du Pont Neuf, 1st
///results.faces.examples

3. Péniche Marcounet
Port des Célestins, Quai de l'Hôtel de Ville, 4th; www.peniche-marcounet.fr
///proud.dangerously.divided

4. Le Mazette
69 Port de la Rapée, 12th;
01 43 45 67 67
///extremes.speared.luring

Théâtre du Châtelet
///detained.owner.shave

Dance at
LE MAZETTE
Head east when things get quieter in central Paris after 12am. This huge bar-boat has DJ sets until 2am most days.

OUTDOORS

Outdoor living is essential to Paris, where apartments are notoriously compact. Manicured parks, cobbled plazas and scenic riversides afford the space and freedom locals relish.

Picnic Spots

As soon as the sun peeks through the clouds, locals grab a blanket and flock to grassy lawns. Picnics embody what Paris is all about: a relaxed pace of life, picturesque settings, great food and perfect company.

JARDIN DU PALAIS ROYAL

Map 1; enter at 8 Rue de Montpensier, 1st; ///runners.twilight.musician
www.domaine-palais-royal.fr

Often overlooked by the crowds who pack into the nearby Louvre, this tree-lined garden offers some unexpected peace and quiet in the 1st. At lunchtime, workers come here to take it easy, lining the benches and tucking into mini picnics of pastries and takeaway coffees. Pull up one of the metal chairs scattered by the central fountain with a book and relax.

PARC DES BUTTES-CHAUMONT

Map 5; enter at Rue Manin and Avenue Secrétan, 19th;
///diverts.revision.asserts

Hot summer weekends are abuzz with crowds of friends packing out this enormous hilltop park. Sun-worshippers while away a whole day here, strolling around the small lake, relaxing with a glass of wine and watching the sun set from the little temple at the top. The park's features are all part of the 19th-century redesign of Paris, but no one balks at the artifice. It feels natural, and that's why it's a firm favourite for picnic gatherings.

PARC MONCEAU

Map 4; enter at Place de la République Dominicaine, 8th; ///gasp.attend.warnings

The only thing posher than the elegant apartments in the 8th arrondissement is this tiny bijou park, where well-heeled groups of girlfriends organize their sophisticated picnics. Decorative ruins and cherry blossom in the spring create an idyllic backdrop for breaking bread on the grass and snapping a photo beside wicker picnic baskets. You may hesitate to leave any crumbs (these are Paris's most genteel grounds, after all), but what's a picnic without them?

» Don't leave without picking up fresh picnic supplies from the nearby Marché des Batignolles if you're visiting on a Saturday.

You won't just stumble upon Jardin Anne Frank *(14 Impasse Berthaud, 3rd)*, a tiny oasis tucked away in the Marais. Surrounded by apartment buildings, it feels like a lost urban playground, manicured but simultaneously a little wild. It pays homage to Anne Frank, making it a tranquil spot to come and contemplate while eating a pastry on a bench.

JARDIN DU LUXEMBOURG

Map 1; enter at Rue de Vaugirard, 6th; ///deputy.bouncing.talking;
www.senat.fr/visite/jardin/index.html

While families settle on the metal chairs that surround the fountains,
a young crowd heads to the grassy knolls at the south of the park –
the only green patch where lounging is permitted. On summer days,
this southern boundary is invaded by students toasting the end of
exams and friends celebrating birthdays, all of them armed with a
bottle of wine and fresh supplies from nearby Marché St-Germain.

PARC DE BERCY

Map 6; 128 Quai de Bercy, 12th; ///studio.because.piles

There's a relaxed residential character to these contemporary gardens,
where those who live nearby come for a post-work catch up on balmy
nights. Located next to the old wine warehouses of Bercy Village,
it's a convenient area to pick up a bottle or two before settling on
the lawns. There are reliable public restrooms available, too, which
means you can broach that extra bottle of wine worry-free.

Try it!
GET GARDENING

If spending all that time in pretty parks has
got your green fingers itching, check out
a gardening workshop at Maison du
Jardinage *(www.jardinons-ensemble.org)*, an
information centre in Parc de Bercy.

PLACE DES VOSGES

Map 2; Place des Vosges, 4th; ///ankle.terms.planting

If the sun's out, expect to fight for a space on the very grounds where royals once jousted (though you'll be armed with baguettes rather than swords). Like the neighbourhood in which it resides, this pretty square attracts an assortment of people: out-of-towners lounging in the sun, families playing in the sand, joggers huffing around the perimeter. There's no better place for a people-watching picnic.

BOIS DE VINCENNES

Map 6; enter at Avenue François Fresneau, 12th;
///casually.foiled.reheat; 01 49 57 15 15

When school's out for summer, families pack the sandwiches and head to this huge country escape. Part of the fun of picnicking here is wandering the paths for a secluded spot on the lake's shoreline – an idyllic spot from which to watch boaters pass. Exploring the adjoining arboretum and château after the picnic is mandatory.

» Don't leave without visiting the Buddhist temple nestled in the park, which offers free meditation sessions to the public.

PLACE LOUIS ARAGON

Map 2; Place Louis Aragon, Île Saint-Louis, 4th; ///locker.ticking.yappy

Sitting at the tip of Île Saint-Louis, this cutesy cobbled terrace is the sunset-watching spot of choice for date nights. Couples cosy up, dangling their legs just a few metres from the Seine below, while boats float by, buskers strum guitars and wine corks pop. Divine.

Urban Adventures

Sure, Parisians have a knack for enjoying a leisurely pace of life, but it's all about balance. The city is an urban playground that tempts everyone to get active and explore (even if only to indulge in a coffee after).

CYCLE THE CANAL

Map 3; start at Port de l'Arsenal, 4th; ///indeed.ember.grudges; www.velib-metropole.fr

Rolling through the city, the breeze in your face as you lazily ride along the river for what seems like hours, is about as local as it gets. But skip the well-trodden Seine trails. Rent a Vélib bike and cycle along the canal from the picturesque Port de l'Arsenal, past picnickers to the green expanse of Parc de la Villette. Don't forget to pack a baguette in your basket to look *really* Parisian.

SAND FABRIK

Map 6; 45 Rue Delizy, Pantin; ///life.together.windy; www.sandfabrik.com

Okay, Sand Fabrik isn't actually outdoors, but we couldn't not include it. After all, this huge, sand-filled room – housed in an old industrial building in Paris's trendy Pantin suburb – is the only place where the

Sand Fabrik's bar-restaurant serves up tasty tapas, burgers and cocktails that are perfect post-workout.

city's beach bums can get their fix of sandy shore year round. Pop in to enjoy a beachy game of volleyball, rugby or badminton with the competitive locals.

RIDE THE BALLON DE PARIS GENERALI

Map 6; Parc André-Citroën, 15th; ///charging.inched.workshops;
www.ballondeparis.com

Once an activity reserved for the upper classes, hot-air ballooning is now open to everyone – and locals are all for it. Seeing the world's largest tethered balloon in the skyline is impressive enough, but viewing the city from an altitude of 150 m (500 ft) from the balloon itself is unparalleled (just ensure it's a fine day, as wind tends to ground it). It's also a tool for raising awareness of air pollution, with blinking lights indicating air quality, so you get a bit of an education, too.

STROLL THE COULÉE VERTE

Map 3; 1 Coulée Verte René-Dumon, 12th; ///dealings.held.water

The inspiration for NYC's highline (despite what New Yorkers might tell you) runs along an old viaduct from Bastille to the Bois de Vincennes. Although some sections dip to ground level, the majority offers a nice elevated hike through the city. It's pretty narrow, so Parisians on their work breaks know not to stop and linger lest they cause a traffic jam, reserving such follies for *les touristes*. You've been warned.

» Don't leave without checking out the artsy shops under the arches at the beginning of the walking route.

JOG THE BOIS DE BOULOGNE

Map 6; Porte Dauphine, 16th; ///trading.infects.hoping

As soon as the sun rises, athletic Parisians head to this beloved patch of greenery, which has become something of a runner's paradise in a city not known for tolerating joggers. For the non-early risers, the paths become afternoon escapes, where exploring the wooded areas and waterfronts is the perfect accompaniment to a calming playlist.

FIND THE PETITE CEINTURE

Map 6; 99 Rue Olivier des Serres, 15th;

///lighter.discouraged.boomed; www.petiteceinture.org

Tucked away in the centre of Paris lies one of its best-kept secrets: an abandoned railway line, its disused tracks overgrown with wild flowers and its tunnels covered in graffiti. While it's slowly being redeveloped into walkable stretches, much of the Petite Ceinture still remains off-limits — though an in-crowd of urban explorers know of the current

Shh!

Occupying the disused former Montrouge-Ceinture station along the Petite Ceinture is Poinçon Paris *(www.poincon paris.com)*, an oft-overlooked spot in the 14th. Colourful dining tables seat hungry lunchers, while exhibitions and concerts draw in a trendy, vibrant crowd. On sunny days, make sure to grab a table on the terrace by the train tracks, while on Sundays, pop by for the energetic "Jazz Brunch".

access points in the 12th, 13th, 15th and 16th arrondissements. Decide which part to explore, then embark on a quiet hike (it can be quite rough at points). Should you need a refreshment, some of the old stations along the line in the north have been turned into cool bars.

SKATE WITH PARI ROLLER

Map 6; start at Place Raoul Dautry, 15th; ///turkeys.quiz.dusted; www.pari-roller.com

Don't be alarmed when you see a rush of skaters flashing by in one protracted wave – it's just another Friday night with Pari Roller, Paris's premier skating event. It's free, so simply rent a pair of skates if you don't have your own and mingle with the hundreds of others laughing and chatting while the music blasts. What more exhilarating way is there to see all of Paris's major landmarks by moonlight?

HIKE THROUGH CIMETIÈRE DU PÈRE LACHAISE

Map 3; enter at Boulevard Ménilmontant, 20th; ///scouting.glad.souk; www.pere-lachaise.com

Cemeteries often instil dread in visitors, but this one is different, with mausoleums to Parisian politicians, artists and writers jutting out of the ground like mini temples. Hilly climbs, crumbling staircases and meandering paths make a walk here more athletic than you'd think; go off-road to get into the really interesting parts.

» **Don't leave without** looking for Jim Morrison's grave (it's a place of pilgrimage for rock fans, so it'll be the most crowded spot).

By the Water

*Paris grew from its river, and locals can hardly
resist the siren's call beckoning them to its edges.
Whether in it, on it or along it, you'll always find
a way to splash around the city's waterways.*

PISCINE MOLITOR

Map 6; 13 Rue Nungesser et Coli, 16th; ///index.directly.petted; www.molitorparis.com/fr

You don't need to be a guest at the hotel attached to this open-air pool to take a dip – much to the delight of well-heeled Parisians. The place to be seen, this Art Deco haven attracts leisure-seekers who sprawl across lounge chairs, sip on cocktails and get pampered in the spa. It's a sophisticated (and splurge) alternative to the crowded public pools, so maybe save it for when your mum or sister are in town.

PARC RIVES DE SEINE

Map 3; start at 2–4 Quai Henri IV, 4th; ///homework.scooter.years

Extending on both sides of the Seine, this riverside park is a favoured local haunt whatever the season. During the summer, it's home to Paris-Plages, a temporary artificial beach paradise that sees students gossiping on deckchairs and large families picnicking under palm

Celebrating? Take a Seine champagne cruise with Ô Chateau for a bit of luxury while sightseeing.

trees. The rest of the year you can expect a post-work crowd unwinding with a large glass of wine in the floating cafés and bars without the crush of crowds.

BASSIN DE L'ARSENAL

Map 3; enter at Place de la Bastille, 12th; ///focus.tablet.began

Linking the Canal Saint-Martin with the Seine, this little port is a popular hangout with a younger, edgier set of Parisians. Join them on a warm evening by grabbing a bottle of wine from nearby Les Caprices de l'Instant before claiming a spot on the cobblestones by the water. It won't be long before you're dreaming of having an apéritif on your own boat, like the many sailors you'll spot.

BASSIN DE LA VILLETTE

Map 5; enter at Quai de la Loire, 19th; ///bright.request.flesh

Lined with cafés, restaurants and two major cinemas, this artificial lake gives off a buzzing festival atmosphere year-round. Picnics and *pétanque* – a winning combination for Parisians – play out day and night on the banks. The warmer weather, meanwhile, brings with it the northern outpost of the city's annual summer beach event, Paris-Plages, with swimming and watersports on offer. Whatever the weather, you can easily spend a day hanging around here if you want to play Parisian (just mind the cycle path, please).

» Don't leave without hiring an electric boat for a cruise, where you'll have access to 40 km (64 miles) of waterways.

Solo, Pair, Crowd

The beauty of Paris is the endless ways you can engage with the water, no matter what you're seeking.

FLYING SOLO

Night walk

Lean up against the railings of Pont Alexandre III, Paris's prettiest and most flamboyant Art Nouveau bridge, to see the city lights reflect in the water at night.

IN A PAIR

Row your boat

Splash along like a set of Pisces in a rowboat on the Lac Inférieur, the largest of the two lakes in the Bois de Boulogne (p166). It's a favourite pastime for Parisians, especially on summer weekends.

FOR A CROWD

It's all fun and games

Les Berges de Seine on the Left Bank was made for families, with walls for climbing and games of hopscotch to keep the kids busy, while parents sip on a coffee from one of the many cafés lining the banks.

PISCINE JOSÉPHINE BAKER

Map 6; Quai François Mauriac, 13th; ///stumpy.solar.spits;
www.piscine-baker.fr

This snazzy public pool actually floats in the Seine – kind of meta, right? It's open all year, but hots up in the summer when the roof rolls back and it's completely outdoors. It's a real community spot, where groups of friends go to cool off, those channelling their inner Joséphine Baker lounge on the sunbeds and kids splash about.

MARNE RIVER

Map 1; depart from Port Solferino, 7th; ///rested.touchy.neutron

Everyone heads to the Seine for boat tours of the big sights, but the Marne, which feeds into the Seine, is a provincial alternative for the nautically minded that few ever venture to navigate. Cruises head east, passing through greenery and locks, to the city's other river. It's a popular route for fans of Impressionism, who can seek the plays of light on the water that inspired the likes of Pissarro and Cézanne.

QUAI FRANÇOIS MAURIAC

Map 6; Quai François Mauriac, 13th; ///contents.search.arming

This riverfront promenade with barge cafés and summertime restaurants is decidedly local. It's the perfect place for a riverside stroll, whether you're catching up with a friend before crossing over to Parc de Bercy or taking your parents to dinner along the banks.

» Don't leave without checking out its most famous occupant, the Batofar, which was the first serious nightclub housed on a boat.

Dreamy Viewpoints

Paris is (rightfully) known as one of the world's most beautiful cities, so it follows that a picturesque view is never hard to find. Everyone has their favourite pocket of the city to watch the sun set or gain perspective.

PARC DE SAINT-CLOUD

Map 6; enter at Avenue de la Grille d'Honneur, Saint-Cloud; ///junior.couple.grills; www.domaine-saint-cloud.fr

Those who live beyond the city limits proudly point out that this is the best place to see Paris in all its glory. Far enough from the inner city to provide sweeping panoramas, Parc de Saint-Cloud soars above the likes of the Eiffel Tower and Montmartre. After work, residents have one vantage point in mind: Rond Point de la Balustrade, to watch the sun set over the Seine.

THE STEPS OF THE SACRÉ-COEUR

Map 4; Parvis du Sacré-Coeur, 18th; ///products.minus.page

Forget climbing to the top of the dome for city views: the steps outside the basilica are where it's at. In the evening, groups of students, local workers and out-of-towners mingle on the steps here, while illicit but welcomed wine and beer vendors weave through

Head here on New Year's Eve for a relaxed street party and great views of fireworks from across the city.

them all selling drinks. It's a chilled spot to catch up while looking out over Paris's rooftops (including the big hitters, like the Notre Dame and Centre Pompidou).

SQUARE DU VERT-GALANT

Map 1; 15 Place du Pont Neuf, 1st; ///stoops.fake.shrimp

Hidden in plain sight at the end of Île de la Cité, this tiny park is one that many Parisians would rather keep to themselves, but it'd be foolish to withhold it. The narrow paths by the water that surround it are filled with revellers who couldn't nab a spot on the park's grassy stretch, but who aren't complaining either — they get the best views of the Louvre. The Parisian whimsy is in full throttle, with sunset ceding to the lights of passing boats as friends and couples soak it all in.

» Don't leave without picking up fresh supplies on your way here for a picnic, because watching the sunset is even better with cheese.

PASSERELLE RICHERAND

Map 5; Passerelle Richerand, Quai de Jemmapes, 10th;
///clubs.swam.coaster

Enticing both serious and budding photographers to rise early is a crowdless sunrise shot of the Canal Saint-Martin. What this footbridge lacks in beauty it makes up for in being the perfect point from which to capture the canal's other elegant bridges while the sun slowly rises above the water. Photos up here are especially striking under a rare covering of winter snow, especially if the water is frozen.

PARC DE BELLEVILLE

Map 5; 11 Rue Piat, 20th; ///racing.walled.beaters

This park isn't the most beautiful – a blessing in disguise for avoiding crowds – but the views from the scruffy hilltop terrace are among the best in Paris. Rewarding the infrequent couples and friend sets who trek to the top of the steep hill are photograph-worthy views of Notre-Dame and the Eiffel Tower on the other side of the city.

» Don't leave without buying some cheap Vietnamese takeout from a restaurant in Belleville for good picnic sustenance while the sun sets.

LAMARCK–CAULAINCOURT

Map 4; Place Dalida, 18th; ///soup.cricket.bucks

Stretching north to the suburbs, the other side of the Butte Montmartre is the less-trodden (read: steeper and more thigh-screaming) alternative to the Sacré-Coeur steps. Proving that gorgeous views don't always equal city-wide panoramas, Lamarck-Caulaincourt is all about the scenic journey, where a walk down the steps passes striped café awnings framing the street as it drops away down the hill.

PONT DE BIR-HAKEIM

Map 6; Pont de Bir-Hakeim, 15th; ///paradise.wider.shape

While out-of-towners scale the Eiffel Tower's full height, locals come to this bridge to see it from a distance – it's the most unobstructed view of the iconic structure you'll find. Nothing says Paris quite like being perched under hanging street lights and looking out over the Iron Lady at night, the occasional metro rattling overhead.

Liked by the locals

"I stop by Parc de Belleville most days, often timing my walk home so I can lean on the railings and watch the Eiffel Tower sparkle at night. There's nowhere better to get a feel for the *quartier*."

ELEANOR JOY, WRITER AND BELLEVILLE RESIDENT

Streets and Squares

Tangles of cobbled roads in hidden districts spill into leafy squares and passages in Paris. These are the threads that hold together the fabric of the city, a geography designed for a **flâneur** *(aimless wanderer).*

BUTTE-AUX-CAILLES

Map 6; 2 Rue de la Butte aux Cailles, 13th; ///trumped.global.swerves

This lesser-known neighbourhood, happily often overlooked by visitors, is loved by locals for its tight-knit community feel. Strolling through feels like wandering a quiet country town, but with an unexpected artistic edge: quirky restaurants line narrow cobblestone lanes, street art fills nearly every corner and laidback bars attract students hoping to bask in the sun. It's all very chill, almost hippy.

GALERIE VIVIENNE

Map 1; 4 Rue des Petits-Champs, 2nd; ///sweeter.year.saying;
www.galerie-vivienne.com

The Neo-Classical shopping arcades built in the 19th century were once the stuff of high society, combining the Parisian pastimes of a *flânerie* and sophisticated shopping trips. These "passages" are few and far between today (no thanks to department stores), but this chic arcade – the best-preserved in Paris – is a firm favourite for those seeking a bit of sophistication and an escape from modern life. An amble on the mosaic floors, a dip into Librairie Jousseaume *(p93)* and a refreshing glass of wine truly transport you to a bygone era.

RUE MONTORGUEIL

Map 1; start at Quartier Montorgueil, 2nd; ///pricing.rates.mass

A buzzing village-like nook in the centre of Paris, this café-lined road has always been a stronghold of community spirit and life. Once a main artery into the former Les Halles market, it remains a food-focused district today, with shops dedicated to French classics drawing both young and old residents. It's the people you meet that shape a visit here, whether it's cheese shop owners with tempting tasting trays in the day or post-work revellers laughing from the restaurant terraces come evening.

» Don't leave without picking up a heavenly pastry from Stoeher, the oldest bakery in Paris, to accompany you on your stroll.

RUE DES BARRES

Map 2; start at Rue François Miron, 4th; ///peachy.crunch.stealing

One of the oldest streets in central Paris, Rue des Barres gives off major history book vibes. A wander through this short passageway is like walking along a timeline: you'll pass half-timbered houses that date back to the 1500s, peek at a church that survived a stray shell from World War I and end up at the Parc Rives de Seine *(p168)*, where modern life plays out at its best.

LA CAMPAGNE À PARIS

Map 6; enter at the stairs, 2–4 Rue Geo Chavez, 20th;
///yell.hurray.drones

It's fitting that the name of this outer district, tucked away in the 20th, translates to "the countryside in Paris". Time seems to stand still in this haven of peace, where you won't find any shops or monuments, simply flower-adorned houses where Parisians live their lives in tranquillity. Few travellers venture this far east, so you'll have it all to yourself (or at least shared with a few locals who, you know, live here).

PASSAGE BRADY

Map 5; 33 Boulevard de Strasbourg, 10th; ///aged.creamed.done

The sweet smell of onions gently browning with fragrant spices is the first sign that you're in the *quartier* often dubbed "Little India". Passage Brady has long been at the heart of the Indian community in Paris – and is loved by locals partial to a good biryani. Unlike other passages prettified for visitors, this one is unpretentious, where 100 types of incense and the sounds of Indian music accompany a stroll through.

RUE DES MARTYRS

Map 4; start S, off Rue Lamartine, 9th; ///bills.reward.gestures

A hot contender for Paris's loveliest street (heck, there's even been a whole book written about it), this sloping lane has become more popular than Parisians would like in recent years. Despite growing gentrification, though, it manages to hold onto its old-school charm. Dedicated residents are to thank for that, who dart between the time-honoured stores along this road every morning, picking up flowers, daily baguettes and the odd roasted chicken from familiar faces. Leisurely ambling through offers a true snapshot of local life.

>> Don't leave without walking to the top of the street to Montmartre's famed *je t'aime* wall, where "I love you" is painted in over 300 languages. Sure, it's been photographed countless times, but it's cute.

PLACE DAUPHINE

Map 1; enter by Rue Henri-Robert, Île de la Cité, 1st; ///referral.careful.stews

Towered over by tall buildings, galleries and restaurants, this triangular-shaped square is secluded enough to feel worlds away from the bustle of the 1st. It might be tiny, but it packs a punch: retirees play *pétanque* on the sandy plaza, dog walkers take to the cobblestone streets surrounding it and lawyers working at the nearby Palace of Justice relax under café awnings. You could circle it five times and never tire of the ambience – it's Paris at its best.

Though many Parisians know of Hôtel Dieu, the oldest hospital in the city, lots of them unknowingly stroll past the inner courtyard that lies just past the entry. Walking through the square feels akin to being in the grounds of an impressive palace, with manicured shrubs surrounding the hospital's Romanesque arches. Visit this pretty square at lunchtime for a leisurely saunter and a slice of calm.

Nearby Getaways

Parisians are incredibly fond of their city, but they're just as much in love with their country. With so many options for day trips from the centre, they're never short of somewhere to go for that breath of fresh air.

CHANTILLY

20 minutes from Gare du Nord station; www.chantilly-tourisme.com

Paris may have won the moniker for the most romantic city, but the couples who flock here on weekend trips would argue otherwise.
A classy combination of château, park and forest, the very fabric of this village was made for romance. Early risers watch the sun come

up over the garden's calm lake, foodies tuck into strawberries with the estate's namesake *crème chantilly*, and country guys and girls at heart stroll the stables – this is the horse-racing capital of France, after all – to catch one of the dressage demonstrations.

AUVERS-SUR-OISE

1 hour from Gare du Nord station

It's hard to tire of Paris's art scene, but when the thought of a stuffy, crowded gallery fills you with dread, this picturesque village – a favourite of the Impressionists – is the perfect antidote. As you stroll the cutesy, quaint streets and the manicured gardens of the Château d'Auvers, it's easy to see why Cézanne and Pissarro were inspired to paint here – and why Van Gogh described it as "seriously beautiful".

» Don't leave without paying a visit to the Église Notre-Dame-de-l'Assomption, the town's picturesque church that was the subject of one of Van Gogh's paintings (now in the Musée d'Orsay).

CHÂTEAU DE VAUX-LE-VICOMTE

1 hour from Gare de l'Est station; www.vaux-le-vicomte.com

Let the out-of-towners take over Versailles; this seriously underrated rural château is a local secret. It's a winner throughout the seasons: in the spring, kids excitedly tackle the Easter egg hunt, while in the summer, groups of girlfriends sip champagne on candlelit evenings. Come winter, it's a playground for all to get into the holiday spirit. Inside, fires crackle, carols play and nutmeg wafts through the air, and as dusk falls, the trees outside light up in what becomes a magical wonderland.

CHARTRES

1.5 hours from Gare du Nord station

Picture a classic, quaint medieval town and you've got Chartres: a towering Gothic cathedral, cobblestone streets lined with half-timbered houses and footbridges spanning the pretty waterside. This is the tranquil day trip Parisians embark on after a long work week, getting swept up in the calm of it all and letting their feet (and mind) wander. Hey, the *flâneur* isn't only found in Paris.

» Don't leave without picking up a Chartres speciality, *le cochelin* – a human-shaped flaky pastry filled with jam.

VITRY-SUR-SEINE

30 minutes from Gare de Lyon

Come the weekend, artsy Parisians head to this grey slice of suburbia south of the city. Why? Well, for one thing, it's the home of MAC/VAL, a contempoary art museum known for its boundary-pushing, avant-garde exhibits, which make some of Paris's other art museums look just a *little* stuffy. For another, there are the cutting-edge plays and dance performances served up by the Jean Vilar theatre. Oh, and did we mention the area's collection of eye-catching murals? Enough said.

PROVINS

1.5 hours from Gare de l'Est station; www.provins.net

This former Roman outpost offers much more than its famous ramparts and towers. Sure, there's plenty of architecture to admire, but the tours of the vaulted underground passages beneath the city

Visit on a Wednesday or Saturday for the market, where you can pick up fresh cheese and seafood. | are where it's at. Dark, spooky and chilly (even in the summer), these tunnels were once warehouses where merchants would store their goods. Bring a jumper.

FONTAINEBLEAU

40 minutes from Gare de Lyon station; www.fontainebleau.fr

Escaping the city hubbub has always been the main reason to visit this ancient royal city: once for the upper classes, now for all walks of life. The château here undoubtedly hogs the headlines, given its 1,500 rooms, all styled over the centuries by various French monarchs. But most Parisians skip it altogether, rather donning their walking boots and heading to the forest that surrounds it – it's the largest natural area of the Île-de-France region. You're likely to pass climbers as you amble through the sun-dappled forest floor, home as it is to tens of thousands of boulders. If you're seeking a thrill, why not give it a go?

SAINT-DENIS

5-minutes from Gare de Nord

Despite a somewhat troubled past, this northern suburb has started to lure in the crowds thanks to its rich history and creative culture. At the Gothic basilica, you can learn all about how Saint-Denis was once the stomping ground of French royalty (countless kings and queens are buried there). Street Art Avenue, meanwhile, shows off the suburb's artistic side: this 5-km (3-mile) stretch along the Canal Saint-Denis is decorated with kaleidoscopically colourful artworks.

**Fantasize through
LA MOUZAÏA**

Finish up with a meander through this small bucolic district of cobbled lanes, picking out your dream home and pretty garden.

5

BLVD SÉRURIER

RUE MANIN

RUE DE CRIMÉE

RUE DU GÉNÉRAL BRUNET

**Midday snack at
PARC DES BUTTES-
CHAUMONT**

Tuck into food with a backdrop of greenery at Pavillon Puebla, then walk it off around the park's romantic lake.

4

RUE BOTZARIS

RUE FESSART

PLACE DES FÊTES

*Renowned French singer-songwriter Edith Piaf was born at **72 Rue de Belleville**, marked now by a plaque above the door.*

BELLEVILLE

3

RUE DE BELLEVILLE

**Mooch around
JOURDAIN**

Stroll through this village-like sub-neighbourhood, window-shopping in the artists' ateliers hidden on Rue de la Villette.

20TH

RUE PIAT

*Lamp-lined alleys like **Passage Plantin** have changed little since Belleville was outside the city limits, before 1860.*

**Enjoy the view from
PARC DE BELLEVILLE**

After climbing to the top of this steep park, settle on the grass and look out to the Eiffel Tower.

2

RUE DES COURONNES

**Amble along the
PETITE CEINTURE**

Go in search of the few walkable sections of the railway that once encircled Paris. It's slowly being reclaimed and is covered in graffiti.

1

11TH

RUE OBERKAMPF

MÉNILMONTANT

0 metres 400
0 yards 400

A morning flânerie through
edgy Belleville

Belleville, as Parisians from other neighbourhoods tend to say, is a *quartier qui bouge:* a lively part of town, as busy at 2am as it is at 10am. It spans two of the most diverse arrondissements, the 19th and 20th, where in the space of a few streets you find yourself walking down forgotten cobblestone lanes, past rows of Chinese supermarkets and alongside locals sporting trendy "looks" that wouldn't be out of place in London's Shoreditch or NYC's Brooklyn. There's nowhere better to see the real Paris and let yourself get lost for the day.

1. La Petite Ceinture
60 Rue de
Ménilmontant, 20th
///terminology.careful.pens

2. Parc de Belleville
11 Rue Piat, 20th
///racing.walled.beaters

3. Jourdain
Rue du Jourdain, 20th
///private.messing.stud

4. Parc des Buttes-Chaumont
1 Rue Botzaris, 19th
///contour.regime.liners

5. La Mouzaïa
///rapid.nail.paraded

72 Rue de Belleville
///took.human.rattler

Passage Plantin
///loyal.marginal.diamonds

With a little research and preparation, this city will feel like a home away from home. Check out these websites to ensure a healthy, safe stay in Paris.

Paris
DIRECTORY

SAFE SPACES

Paris is generally a welcoming city, but should you feel uneasy at any point or want to find your community, there are spaces catering to different genders, sexualities, demographics and religions.

www.centrelgbtparis.org
Centre running events and offering support for the LGBTQ+ community.

www.cjl-paris.org
Jewish community centre led by the first female rabbi of France.

www.espacesantetrans.fr
Project to improve healthcare for trans people in France, with a helpline.

www.icsparis.com
A non-profit offering mental health support for English speakers.

www.inter-lgbt.org
Organizers of the annual Paris Pride.

HEALTH

Healthcare in France is pricey, so take out comprehensive health insurance; EU residents can register for a European Health Insurance Card (EHIC) and UK citizens can apply for the UK Global Health Insurance Card (GHIC) to get discounted or free care. If you do need medical assistance, there are many pharmacies and hospitals across town.

www.3237.fr
Pharmacies open outside normal hours.

www.ameli.fr
Official portal for healthcare in France.

www.american-hospital.org
Paris's largest English-speaking hospital.

www.doctolib.fr
Book appointments with local clinics, including dentists and doctors.

https://paris.croix-rouge.fr
Red Cross, an English-friendly clinic with sexual health testing and advice.

www.sosmedecins.fr/en
24/7 home visits for situations not requiring an ambulance; call-out fees from €35.

TRAVEL SAFETY ADVICE

Before you travel – and while you're here – always keep tabs on France's latest regulations.

www.diplomatie.gouv.fr
Information from the French government on travelling to, and living in, France.

www.gov.uk/foreign-travel-advice
Up-to-date travel advice from the FCDO.

www.gouvernement.fr
The French government website, the first port of call for COVID-19 regulations.

www.prefecturedepolice. interieur.gouv.fr
The Préfecture's tips for staying safe and what to do if you're a victim of crime.

www.solidaritefemmes.org
Resources and a helpline for female victims of violence.

ACCESSIBILITY

Provision for those with reduced mobility remains very poor in Paris, particularly on public transport. The below websites provide useful resources to make exploring the city easier.

www.g7.fr
Company offering accessible taxis for those with specific requirements.

www.handicap.monuments-nationaux.fr
French-only information for people with specific requirements when visiting sites.

www.jaccede.com/en
Crowd-sourced details of accessible museums, bars, restaurants and cinemas.

www.parisinfo.com
Official resource for visiting Paris, with an annually updated downloadable guide for travelling with specific requirements.

www.ratp.fr
Information on public transport options for those with reduced mobility or impaired sight.

INDEX

1st arrondissement 14, 18
2nd arrondissement 14, 18
3rd arrondissement 14, 20
4th arrondissement 14, 20
5th arrondissement 14, 20
6th arrondissement 14, 18
7th arrondissement 14, 18
8th arrondissement 14, 24
9th arrondissement 15, 24
10th arrondissement 15, 26
11th arrondissement 15, 22
12th arrondissement 15, 22
13th arrondissement 15, 28
14th arrondissement 15, 28
15th arrondissement 15, 28
16th arrondissement 15, 28
17th arrondissement 15, 24
18th arrondissement 15, 24
19th arrondissement 15, 26
20th arrondissement 15, 26
59 Rivoli 112–13, 132, 133
72 Rue de Belleville 184, 185
104 Centquatre 128

A
À la Folie Paris 146–7
À la Ville de Rodez 36, 83
accessibility 187
Agrology 152
Ailleurs 90
Aki Boulangerie 33
apéritif spots 152–5
arrondissements 14–15
Arts 9, 11, 106–33
Asian Quarter 15
Atelier C 52, 53
Atelier des Lumières 114, 132, 133
Au P'tit Grec 39
Aujourd'hui Demain 51

Auvers-sur-Oise 181
Avenue Montaigne 104, 105

B
Back in Black 57
Baieta 46–7
Ballon de Paris Generali 165
BAPBAP Brewery 70
Bar à Iode Saint Germain 45
Bar Gallia 71
Bar Hemingway 76, 77
barge bars 137
bars and cafés 54–77, 136–9, 145–7, 152–5
Bassin de la Villette 169
Bassin de l'Arsenal 169
Bastille 165
Bastille Day 9
Batignolles district 15
beaches, artificial 164–5, 169
beauty shops 100–103
beer 68–71
Belleville 15, 184–5
Benoît Castel 34
Bisou 64
Bistrot Paul Bert 41, 52, 53
Black Paris Walks, Le Paris Noir 126
BMK 82
Bo & Mie 34
Bois de Boulogne 166, 170
Bois de Vincennes 163, 165
book shops 82–5
Bouillon Racine 47
Boulangerie Bo 32–3, 52, 53
boules 144–5
Bowling de Paris Front de Sein 147
Brasserie Auteuil 138
Brasserie de la Goutte d'Or 68

Breathe Restaurant 50
breweries 68–71
Butte-aux-Cailles 176

C
Café Chéri(e) 64
Café Chilango 42
Café du Coin 153
Café Pimpin 59
Caféothèque 59
Canal Saint-Martin 139, 148–9, 169, 173
candle-making 88
Cantine Primeur 48
Centre Pompidou 108–9, 138, 173
Champs-Élysées 14, 105
Chantilly 180–81
Chartres 182
Château de Vaux-le-Vicomte 181
Chercheminippes 96
Chez Alain Miam Miam 38–9
Chez Bouboule 144–5
Chez Prune 56
CheZaline 36–7
Christmas 9
Cimitière du Père Lachaise 167
Ciné Le Grand Action 120–21
Cinéma en Plein Air 120
Cirque Electrique 142–3
Cité de l'Architecture et du Patrimoine Palais du Tokyo 110
classes 34, 80, 88, 150, 162
clothes shops 96–9, 104–5
clubs 121, 140–42
cocktail joints 64–7, 76–7, 139
coffee shops 56–9

Coinstot Vino 60
community projects 128–31
Comptoir des Archives 73
Confiture Parisienne 80
cookery classes 34, 80
Coulée Verte 165
Cravan 154
Crypte Archeologique de l'Île de la Cité 125
CSAO 90, 91
culture 9, 11, 106–33
cycling 12, 163

D

dance 123, 137, 139, 141, 150–51
day trips 180–83
Dev!ant 61
dinners, cosy 40–43
Dirty Lemon 65
Domaine la Bouche du Roi 69
drink 10, 54–77
Driving 13

E

E. Dehillerin 82
Early June 40
Écoles Cinéma Club 122
Edwart Chocolatier 83
Église St Sulpice 143
Eiffel Tower 69, 109, 149, 151, 172, 174, 175, 184
Elmer 46
Esprit 50cl 65

F

Faguo 97
festivals 8, 9
film 120–23
Fleux 89
Fondation Cartier pour l'Art Contemporain 115
Fondation Louis Vuitton 114–15
Fontainebleau 183
food 9, 10, 30–53, 80–83

formules, top 44–7
Freddy's 62
Fulgurances "L'Adresse" 45

G

Galerie Perrotin 112
Galerie Vivienne 176–7
game night 144–7
Gamelle 146
gardening workshops 162
Gossima Ping Pong Bar 146
gourmet shops 80–83
Goutte d'Or (Little Africa) 15
Grand Mosquée de Paris 73
Grand Rex 122
Grill Room 47
Gros Bao 39
Ground Control 131, 132, 133
guinguettes 136–9, 146–7

H

Halle Saint-Pierre 113
Hanoï Corner 57
Harry's New York Bar 76, 77
Haut Marais 14
health 186–7
history 124–7
homeware stores 88–91
Hood, The 58
Hôtel Dieu 179
Huygens 101

I

Institut du Monde Arabe 125
Isakin 99

J

Jah Jah By Le Tricycle 48–9
Jardin Anne Frank 161
Jardin du Carousel 151
Jardin du Luxembourg 162
Jardin du Palais Royal 160
Jardin Nelson Mandela 151
Jardin Tino-Rossi 150–51

jogging 166
Jourdain 184, 185

K

KB 74
Kiliwatch 98–9

L

La Belle Hortense 60–61
La Bellevilloise 140–41
La Campagne à Paris 178
La Commune 67
La Fine Mousse 70–71
La Fontaine 154
La Gare 142
La Javelle 139
La Maison du Pastel 114, 132, 133
La Marine 74–5
La Mouzaïa 184, 185
La Mutinerie 130, 131
La Place Verte 75
La Rotonde Stalingrad 75
La Sardine 72–3
La Seine Musicale 149
La Trésorerie 89
La Vigne de Suresnes 69
La Winerie Parisienne 69
L'Abattoir Végétal 50
Lady Long Solo 95
Lamarck–Caulaincourt 174
Latin Quarter 14
Lavomatic 67
Le Bal 113
Le Bar à Pintes 145
Le Baron Rouge 52, 53, 62
Le Cadoret 42
Le Chalet Savoyard 40–41
Le Dernier Bar avant la Fin du Monde 147
Le Divan du Monde 121
Le Foyer de la Madeleine 44
Le Georges 138
Le Hasard Ludique 131

Le Klub 142
Le Labo 152–3
Le Louxor 123
Le Marais 14
Le Mazette 141, 157
Le Pacifique 42
Le Pavillon des Canaux 58
Le Perchoir Ménilmontant 136
Le Petit Fer à Cheval 154
Le Progrès 72
Le Récho's 129
Le Recyclerie 128–9
Le Shakirail 129
Le Syndicat 76, 77
Le Top du Point Ephémère 139
Le Vin au Vert 81
L'Eau les Rèves 95
L'École des Arts Joailliers 105
Legay Choc 33
Les Berges de Seine 170
Les Cinq Toits 129
Les Cuves de Fauve 68–9
Les Mots à la Bouche 94
Les Philosophes Café 74
Less Is More 97
LGBTQ+ scene 136–7, 186
Librairie Galignani 92
Librairie Jousseaume 93
Liquides Bar à Parfum 100–101
Little Red Door 65
Little Tokyo 14
L'Officine Universelle Buly 103
Loox 103
Lulu White 67
lunch on the go 36–9

M

Mad Lords 99
Maison du Jardinage 162
Maison Européenne de la
    Photographie 115
Maison Plisson 81
Mama Shelter East 137
Mamiche 35

maps 16–29
Marché aux Puces de la Porte
    de Vannes 86
Marché Biologique des
    Batignolles 87
Marché d'Aligre 15, 52, 53, 84
Marché Dejean 87
Marché des Enfants Rouges 38
Marché Président-Wilson 84–5
Marché Saint-Martin 85
Marché Saint-Pierre 85
markets 9, 15, 38, 52, 53, 84–7
Marlusse et Lapin 76, 77
Marne River 171
Ménilmontant 15
Merci 90
Mieux 44–5
modern art 112–15
Mokoloco 38
Montmartre 15, 172
Montparnasse 15
Moonshiner 67
Moulin Rouge 76, 77
Mr Alphonse 62
Musée Carnavalet 124
Musée d'Art et d'Histoire du
    Judaïsme 124–5
Musée de Cluny 119
Musée de l'Illusion 118
Musée de Montmartre 119
Musée des Arts et Métiers 111
Musée des Arts Forains 117
Musée d'Orsay 109
Musée du Louvre 110–11, 156,
    157
Musée du Luxembourg 108
Musée du Quai Branly–
    Jacques Chirac 116
Musée Edith Piaf 118–19
Musée Gustave Moreau 132,
    133
Musée Jacquemart-André 117
Musée Nationale de l'Histoire
    de l'Immigration 127

Musée Rodin 127
Musée Yves Saint Laurent 104,
    105
museums and galleries 9, 104,
    105, 108–19, 124–7
music 8, 140–43
musicals 122, 123

N

Naked Shop 102–3
New Soul Food 37
nightlife 11, 134–57
Nose 102
Notre-Dame 125, 173, 174

O

Oh My Cream! 101
open-air living rooms 148–51
Opéra district 15
outdoor activities 8, 11, 158–85

P

Palais Galliera 111
Palais Royale 105
Paname Brewing Company
    70
Panthéon 126–7
Papier Plus 92–3
Papier Tigre 94
Parc de Belleville 174, 175, 184,
    185
Parc de Bercy 162
Parc de la Villette 120, 146, 164
Parc de Saint-Cloud 172
Parc des Buttes-Chaumont
    160–61, 184, 185
Parc du Champ-de-Mars 149
Parc Monceau 161
Parc Rives de Seine 166–7, 177
Pari Roller 167
Paris-Plages 169
parks and gardens 120, 146,
    149, 150–51, 160–63, 170,
    172, 174–5

Passage Brady 178
Passerelle Richerand 173
patisseries 32–5
Pavillon Puebla 139
Péniche Marcounet 137, 156, 157
pétanque 144, 148, 169
Petite Ceinture 166–7, 184, 185
Philharmonie de Paris 143
picnics 8, 160–63, 169
Pigalle 15
Pignon 153
Pinball Museum 118
Piscine Joséphine Baker 171
Piscine Molitor 168
Pizza Julia 49
Place Dauphine 179
Place des Vosges 163
Place du Marché Sainte-
    Catherine 149
Place Louis Aragon 163
Poinçon Paris 166
Pompette 61
Pont Alexandre III 170
Pont d'Alma 104, 105
Pont de Bir-Hakim 174
Pont des Arts 150
Port de 'Arsenal 164
Potager de Charlotte 51
Pozzetto 58
Présence Africaine 93
Provins 182–3
public transport 12–13

Q

Quai de la Loire 144, 148
Quai de l'Hôtel de Ville 132,
    133
Quai François Mauriac 171

R

Red Wheelbarrow 95
Reset 145
restaurants 40–53
Ritz, The 76, 77

Rocky Horror at Studio
    Galande 121
rooftops 136–9
Rooster 46
Rosa Bonheur 136
Rouje 98
Rue des Barres 177
Rue des Martyrs 178–9
Rue Montorgueil 177

S

Sacha Finkelsztajn 32
Sacré Coeur 172–3
safety 186
Saint Germain 14
Saint-Denis 183
Sand Fabrik 164–5
Season Square 50–51
seasons 8–9
Seine, River 8–9, 137, 140, 147,
    150, 156–7, 168–71
Sergeant Paper 88–9
Shakespeare and Company 94
Shinzo 96–7
shopping 9, 10–11, 78–105,
    176–7
smoking 11
Square du Vert-Galant 156,
    157, 173
stationery shops 82–5
Steps of the Sacré-Coeur
    172–3
street style 96–9
Supersonic 141
swimming 168, 169, 171

T

Taka & Vermo 81
Tango Argentin 150
taxis 13
tennis 8
Terrass" Hotel 138
Terrasses 72–5, 136
Théâtre de la Ville de Paris 123

Théâtre du Châtelet 123, 156,
    157
Théâtre Mogador 122
theatres 120–23
Tien Hiang 49
tipping 11
Tours
    cocktail culture 76–7
    edgy Belleville 184–5
    food in the 12th 53–4
    haute couture 104–5
    Paris's art scene 132–3
    Seine path 156–7
transport 12–13
travel safety advice 187
Treize au Jardin 59

U

Urfa Dürüm 37
Utopie 35

V

Valois Vintage 104, 105
Vegetarian/Vegan food
    48–51
Velan 82–3
VG Patisserie 35
Viaduc des Arts 52, 53
viewpoints 172–5
Vignerons Parisiens 71
Village Saint-Paul 86–7
Vitry-sur-Seine 182

W

walking 12, 165, 166–7
Waly Fay 41
water activities 168–71
water, drinking 11
wine 9, 81
wine Bars 60–63
wineries 68–71

Y

Yellow Tucan 56

ACKNOWLEDGEMENTS

Meet the illustrator

*Award-winning British illustrator
David Doran is based in a studio by the sea
in Falmouth, Cornwall. When not drawing
and designing, David tries to make the
most of the beautiful area in which he's
based; sea-swimming all year round,
running the coastal paths and generally
spending as much time outside as possible.*

With thanks

*DK Eyewitness would like to thank the
following people for their contribution
to the first edition of this book: Yuki
Higashinakano, Bryan Pirolli, Lucy
Richards, Tania Gomes, Zoë Rutland
and Casper Morris.*

MIX
Paper | Supporting
responsible forestry
FSC
www.fsc.org
FSC™ C018179

This book was made with
Forest Stewardship Council™
certified paper – one small
step in DK's commitment to
a sustainable future.
**For more information go to
www.dk.com/our-green-pledge**

A NOTE FROM DK EYEWITNESS

The world is fast-changing and it's keeping us folk at
DK Eyewitness on our toes. We've worked hard to ensure
that this edition of Paris Like a Local is up-to-date and
reflects today's favourite places but we know that standards
shift, venues close and new ones pop up in their place. So, if
you notice something has closed, we've got something
wrong or left something out, we want to hear about it.
Please drop us a line at travelguides@dk.com

Penguin
Random
House

THIS EDITION UPDATED BY

Contributors Yuki Higashinakano
Senior Editor Lucy Richards
Senior Designer Stuti Tiwari
Project Editor Rachel Laidler
Project Art Editor Bharti Karakoti
Designer Jordan Lambley
Indexer Helen Peters
Senior Cartographic Editor Casper Morris
Cartography Manager Suresh Kumar
Jacket Designer Sarah Snelling
Jacket Illustrator David Doran
Senior Production Editor Jason Little
Senior Production Controller Samantha Cross
Managing Editor Hollie Teague
Managing Art Editors Sarah Snelling,
Priyanka Thakur
Art Director Maxine Pedliham
Publishing Director Georgina Dee

First edition 2021
Published in Great Britain by Dorling Kindersley Limited,
DK, One Embassy Gardens, 8 Viaduct Gardens,
London SW11 7BW.

The authorised representative in the EEA is
Dorling Kindersley Verlag GmbH. Arnulfstr.
124, 80636 Munich, Germany.

Published in the United States by DK Publishing,
1745 Broadway, 20th Floor, New York, NY 10019.

Copyright © 2021, 2023 Dorling Kindersley Limited
A Penguin Random House Company
22 23 24 25 10 9 8 7 6 5 4 3 2 1

The publishers cannot accept responsibility for any consequences arising from
the use of this book, nor for any material on third party websites, and cannot
guarantee that any website address in this book will be a suitable source of
travel information.

A CIP catalog record for this book is available from the British Library.
A catalog record for this book is available from the Library of Congress.
ISSN: 1542 1554
ISBN: 978 0 2415 6904 7
Printed and bound in China.
www.dk.com